GET YOUR REAR INTO GEAR

Job Searching Tips for Career Success

ALY BANNISTER

AF472317

Copyright © 2020 Aly Bannister
First published in Australia in 2020
by Karen McDermott
Waikiki, WA 6169

All rights reserved. No part of this book may be used or reproduced by any means, graphic, electronic, or mechanical, including photocopying, recording, taping or by any information storage retrieval system without the written permission of the copyright owner except in the case of brief quotations embodied in critical articles and reviews.

Although the author and publisher have made every effort to ensure that the information in this book was correct at press time, the author and publisher do not assume and hereby disclaim any liability to any party for any loss, damage, or disruption caused by errors or omissions, whether such errors or omissions result from negligence, accident, or any other cause.

Interior design: Ida Jansson
Cover Art Work: KMD Books
Cover photo: Diana Henderson Life as Art
Editor: Dannielle Line.

National Library of Australia Cataloguing-in-Publication data:
Get Your Rear into Gear/Aly Bannister
Success/Self-help

ISBN: 978-0-6489733-0-0 (sc)

ISBN: 978-0-6489733-1-7 (e)

CONTENTS

A Note from Aly 7
Dedication 9
Introduction 15
Preface 25

Tip 1: Get Your Rear into Gear - N.O.W. 31
Tip 2: Proofread, proofread, and proofread again! 35
Tip 3: Start with a Spirit of Optimism 40
Tip 4: Build your Employer Wish List - WHO and WHY 42
Tip 5: Identify Your Non-Negotiable List 49
Tip 6: Collate your Foundation Documents 52
Tip 7: Conduct Research before preparing your Resume 57
Tip 8: Have Multiple Resumes 59
Tip 9: Build a Winning Resume 61
Tip 10: Resume Header - Essential Ingredients 63
Tip 11: Build an enticing Elevator Pitch 66
Tip 12: Professional Profile: Bonus Tip 68
Tip 13: Include the Employer Core Values 69
Tip 14: Quality trumps Quantity 70
Tip 15: Short, Sweet, and to the Point 71

Tip 16: No photographs please 73
Tip 17: Include Key Achievements 74
Tip 18: Be the solution to the problem 77
Tip 19: Build your answers with Acronyms 78
Tip 20: Max out the Power Verbs 80
Tip 21: Build an appealing Career History 83
Tip 22: Don't tell Porky Pies 84
Tip 23: Keep it real 85
Tip 24: Bullet Point Key Responsibilities 87
Tip 25: Do not copy and paste your job description 89
Tip 26: Include only relevant Education and Qualifications 90
Tip 27: People buy people. Help employers 'buy into your skills' 92
Tip 28: Employability Skills – What are they? 94
Tip 29: Highlight Key Skills 97
Tip 30: References and Referees 101
Tip 31: Hobbies and Interests, or space saver? 103
Tip 32: Select the resume to fit your needs 104
Tip 33: How to beat the ATS 107
Tip 34: Create a professional voice message 108
Tip 35: Resume checklist 110
Tip 36: Creative Cover Letters 112
Tip 37: The Hidden Job Market 118
Tip 38: Referrals. 'It's not what you know, it's who you know.' 124
Tip 39: Think like a Recruitment Consultant 126
Tip 40: Connect with a Recruitment Consultant 130
Tip 41: Get onboard with LinkedIn in twelve easy steps 134
Tip 42: Failing to Plan is Planning to Fail 139
Tip 43: What do I need to succeed? 143

Tip 44: Employer Contact List and Vacancy Tracker 148
Tip 45: Craft Your Career Goals 150
Tip 46: The 7 P's and Interview Preparation 154
Tip 47: Preparation Builds Confidence 157
Tip 48: Phone Interviews 161
Tip 49: Face-to-Face Interviews 163
Tip 50: Be comfortable selling your skills 166
Tip 51: Common interview Q and A's 168
Tip 52: Questions to ask at the interview 171
Tip 53: Describe your achievements 172
Tip 54: Fake it 'til you make it 174
Tip 55: Be kind to yourself 178
Tip 56: Remove the negative self-chatter 183
Tip 57: Reward your efforts 186
Tip 58: Rinse and Repeat method 189
Tip 59: Attitude – pick a good one 191
Tip 60: Faith, Courage and Discipline 193

Testimonials *199*
About Aly *215*
Useful websites to consider in Australia *217*

Acknowledgement

With my greatest thanks to Karen McDermott of KMD Books, a true friend, mentor and all round incredible human being. Without your guidance and belief in me, this book would not have been possible. I am forever in your debt. Thank you x

To my husband, Jay, Your unwavering support, love, kindness and total conviction in my writing and coaching abilities has spurred me on - again. Thank you. I love you and our boys so much, Connor, Jacob and Noah x x x

To my mum, Sadie Donaghy, this is my I.O.U. to you. Now, as a mother, I get it! All of my love, and eternal respect x

A NOTE FROM ALY

Thank you!

I am truly grateful you have invested in yourself and your future. It's my guess you've bought this book because you want to become more successful finding a job, re-entering the workforce or progressing with your future career aspirations. I genuinely hope and believe that over the next 200+ pages you will find the content advantageous, ideally leading you to finding a rewarding job that you enjoy and one that ticks all of your boxes. It's been written from the heart with the sole aim of giving you more confidence in your own job seeking abilities. Therefore, enabling you to become a more independent job seeker, having learnt where to start and how to find employment others may not have considered. My overarching aspiration is this:

By the end of the book, you will feel more informed about the whole job searching experience. You will have a clearer understanding of what you need to succeed, leaving you feeling more empowered, better equipped, and completely prepared to conquer the entire process. Thus improving your job searching methods and ultimately your chances of success in today's job market.

And it is just that... a process! Just like any other process. At first, it's a technique that must be learned, then practised and finally perfected along the way. You will often hear me say "Practice leads to development." No one is expecting you to get it right first time, although some do. But remember this: You cannot fail. You can only learn!

Take the pressure off yourself a little. I have found many job seekers become exasperated in the early stages on their quest for employment because they are not experiencing immediate success. They then give up the process entirely, leaving themselves feeling demotivated and frustrated, possibly in a job they don't like or enjoy. Even worse, unemployed for lengthy periods of time. Hang on in there… that's what I say! Be patient, back yourself, and the results will come. Your endurance will pay off big time!

I have seen the positive results thousands of job seekers have achieved. Effectively, it's a reward for their tenacious approach and dedication. Even as I'm writing this book, as a full-time Career Coach, many of the clients I work with daily are finding increased levels of success week in, week out. There are lots of opportunities available for you. But first, you must be prepared to accomplish the results you are aiming for. As I'm sure you already know, it is normal to procrastinate sometimes over things we don't enjoy. Well, not anymore. Now is the time to ***Get Your Rear into Gear.***

DEDICATION

To Mum

And to all other mums, job seekers young and old entering or re-entering the workforce. You are better than you realise!

I will be forever grateful for having such a loving mother. I dedicate this book to my mum, who never really re-entered the workforce after having children. Why didn't she just go back to work? Because she lost a great deal of her confidence regarding her own skills and abilities in the workplace. She felt insecure and I would even go further and say she became anxious at the thought of going back to work. But she is, by far, not on her own.

As a young girl, I never really understood why my mother didn't have a career, regular part-time or full-time job, a normal place of work to where she would routinely go. Now, as a mature woman, mother, wife and professional Career Coach, I completely understand. I truly get it!

After having children, your life changes in ways you could never imagine. You can lose some of your self-confidence and the belief in your own skills and abilities because you are no longer a regular participant of the daily workforce. Often, mums are left with large gaps in the career history part of their resume. It can even feel like you have already missed out on so much (in-house training, a promotion, industry insights, the latest jargon, pay, benefits, feeling like part of the team or crew etc. etc.) Especially after taking a career break. It can seem difficult to take the first step or make the big leap back into work.

Heaps of my clients, who are also mothers, have described feeling insecure about their abilities. This does not apply to all mums re-entering the workforce. However, there are many women who do feel like this. I seem to work with lots of them who tell me this kind of story repeatedly (I think I draw mums towards me, which makes me happy).

Even as an extremely confident person myself, I, too, lost a little confidence when I re-entered the workforce after my first son was born. I still wanted to be recognised for the value I brought to the office, and be appreciated for the knowledge I could share, along with the experience and additional benefits I could bring to the team. But it's pretty hard to do when you are functioning on two to four hours sleep per night, and your hormones are all over the place. Remembering your own name some days is a bonus.

It's normal to feel like crying because you're so exhausted. I always related my priorities and thoughts to getting my baby ready for day-care and packing my little one's clothes and nappies, food and teething gel before work. My personal needs were firmly at the bottom of the list of things needing to be done before catching the train to work. You know, little things like breakfast. Before work? I don't think so. My son needed to be at day-care for 6.45am, in readiness for me to be on the 7.05am train to the city. Getting to work after travelling an hour by car and then train was enough of a challenge without having to contemplate what was I going to eat for my breakfast.

So, yes, I totally understand why my mother, and so many other mums, choose never to return to their original career or job after having a family.

My confidence took a huge knock after having a baby. But somehow, I overcame the nerves. Some of us struggle under pressure. Some of us excel. Whilst I found it extremely challenging at times, I loved buying a cup of coffee for myself and going to the toilet on my own without having to bring baby everywhere with me. Yes, you heard me right. I found that a real bonus of returning to the workplace. I really enjoyed being back in the office after maternity leave. I loved the camaraderie amongst my colleagues and the Friday night socials. It helped me to feel like Aly again, and not just a mum.

However, like many other mums, my mother decided she would rather be a full-time, stay-at-home mum and not return to work. Therefore, she dedicated her attention and time to raising me and my three siblings. I believe if she had the opportunity to realise her full potential, after having her career break, she would have returned to work whether it was part-time or full-time in those early days of being a mum. Yet, like lots of other mums of the 60s/70s generation, she didn't have a solid career, so never went back into steady employment. She did have a casual, part-time catering assistant job to earn a little extra cash on a Saturday at the local gala. In hindsight, I know that given the opportunity again, she would have re-entered the workforce in a heartbeat. If she only had a little more faith in her own abilities, a clearer understanding of the value she could bring to a job, or someone to tell her that she had everything required to re-enter the workforce. She only needed a bit of encouragement and pointing in the right direction.

The decision to not go back to work was one I think she regretted over the years, especially when she got older. Inevitably, us kids grew up and left home when she was still of a working age. I believe she felt she'd lost some of her sense of purpose. If I knew then what I know now, I would have loved to have helped her find a job. That's why I have such a huge soft spot for mums trying to re-enter the workforce today.

Today I help a variety of clients re-enter the workforce. But in particular, I find there are many women facing the same dilemma as my mum was. They struggle to find adequate employment after having kids. Asking themselves, *Should I go back to work? Will my skills be recognised? Am I good enough? Where do I start after being out of the workforce for so long? I'm not sure which direction to go in? Are there any well-paid part-time jobs out there? Is it possible to strike a positive work-life balance to fit in around my family needs? What should I put on my resume about having a break? Are my skills still relevant?*

Most mums who I meet in workshops tell me they have lost some or all of their (work-related) confidence. Some mums I work with are happy to settle for less and take a lower-paid job to fit in with an employer and their family just to get by.

After a few sessions together, more often than not, each comes to the realisation they have so much to offer an employer. They don't have to take any old job to fit in with an employer's needs. Yes, there has to be some flexibility on both sides. But there is still fulfilment to be found in part-time or full-time roles with good companies. There are still opportunities available where they can aim towards creating a positive work-life balance. You can too!

I genuinely believe, even in today's job market, you can drive your own success and have a purposeful career and a happy home life whilst still meeting an employer's expectations.

I have partnered with many clients, both male and female, and they have easily regained their confidence after learning some 'tips and tricks' of job searching. But above all, they realise they can achieve great things in their careers—at any age.

My mother was an amazing lady who was always there for

me. She dedicated her life to our family and made sacrifices I only realised after becoming a mum myself. Her dedication to us and time away from the workforce made a huge impact on her self-confidence and earning capacity. She sacrificed a great deal and I now feel it is my duty to repay her selflessness with my debt of gratitude. And to help as many other mums and job seekers of all ages, backgrounds and circumstances on this planet to find and secure a fulfilling job, part-time or full-time employment and/or a rewarding career.

It doesn't matter if you're a young or more mature job seeker, a mum or a dad re-entering the workforce, or a person with no kids. Or whether you're a seasoned job seeker, a career-changer or a school kid, a person whose been made redundant, a uni graduate or school leaver. You all have great skills!

You are better than you realise. You are the 'Boxer and I'm your Corner Man.' With a bit of direction, you can go the distance and achieve great things. You and your future employer will see your value! Let's get your confidence, knowledge and job searching skills 'up to scratch' and right where they need to be, so you become better prepared for the exciting opportunities that lie ahead of you.

Thank you for allowing me to be in your corner xxx

INTRODUCTION

What is a Career Coach, and how can one help you?

Career Coaches can help people with a wide variety of career-related goals and services.

Usually, clients (job seekers) can reasonably expect to gain career confidence, insights, encouragement, and inspiration when engaging the services of a Career Coach. They should also feel as though the coaching relationship enables them to relax a bit more. The job searching process can create a fair amount of anxiety, fear, and vulnerability in some. My aim is to remove some pressure a job seeker may be experiencing.

When I meet a client, I work towards establishing a rapport to find some common ground, to help them relax, and put them at ease to get the best out of them. It then becomes clearer which factors may keep them stuck in their careers, or what is holding them back from looking for a job.

Some job seekers choose a Career Coach because they're stuck in a dead-end job that brings no meaning or purpose to their lives. Others are challenged by the demands of striking a positive work/life balance. Many clients are looking to build a career again after having a family. Others have a demanding role and want to change jobs to create a more harmonious work-life balance.

Not everyone knows exactly what they want to achieve initially, or what they want to do with their lives, so need help developing and executing a career plan to get where they want. Others have a crystal-clear picture of what they want to achieve but aren't sure how to go about it. Many just want to learn how to find a job and improve their ongoing job searching strategies to enhance their performance and ultimately their success rate in the future.

Career coaching can help job seekers/clients with these services and more.

Career Coaches typically have experience and training in a variety of career development strategies, including:

- Career exploration
- Interview preparation and performance coaching
- Creative job search strategies
- Resume writing
- Cover letters
- Addressing Key Selection Criteria
- Career, personality and strengths assessments
- Personal marketing and branding
- Evaluating prospective employers
- Salary negotiations
- Building confidence techniques

Some professionals are referred to as a Career Practitioner, Career Advisor, Career Development Specialist or Career Coach.

I'm a Career Coach. One analogy I frequently use to describe what I do is this:

'You are the Boxer. I'm your Corner Man.' I've got your back!

My area of expertise as a Career Coach is to help individuals like you to build more confidence and become better prepared to find and secure employment independently. 'Independently' being the key word here. It's my intention to show you how to replicate the techniques I've learnt over many years, which have proven to be successful. This way, you can easily implement your own plan and execute your own strategy with almost no assistance in the future.

Even though it is tempting to secure employment on behalf of a client sometimes, I have to pull myself back from doing it. Because whilst I love helping clients to find a job, by carrying out that service, such as securing employment on behalf of a job seeker, it's doing them a disservice. If I do it on their behalf, the action is effectively telling my client I don't have enough confidence in your ability to do it for yourself, thereby doing the job seeker a complete disservice. The opposite of what a coach should be doing. Think about a football coach. He shouts instructions from the sideline. He's not on the field playing the game. Well, it's the same with Career Coaching.

A job seeker can only build self-esteem and confidence if you encourage them to do it for themselves rather than constantly doing something for them. Otherwise I would be giving a person the wrong message and realistically not giving the individual an advantage in the long term.

A good Career Coach should help enlighten you and enable you to do things for yourself by sharing knowledge, guidance, tips and information (like the guy sitting outside the corner of the boxing ring—albeit shouting advice and instructions). I'm a little gentler in my approach.

In fact, if I continue to find employment for others, I become a Recruitment Service rather than a Career Coach. Someone who should help a client become more informed about new techniques, strategies and how to leverage upon opportunities in today's job market.

It is my belief everyone can learn how to find and secure

employment for themselves, requiring just a little help and guidance in the right direction. You the job seeker might need to build tenacity, build broad shoulders or put your 'Big Girl Pants' on. Prepare yourself to be relentless and not give up until you have conquered the process, eventually winning the day.

There is a marvellous quote by: Esther Hicks from the Law of Attraction.

"The greatest gift you could ever give to another is your highest expectation of their success!"

I have great expectations of you. I expect you to be successful whether it's a tough job market or not. I believe in you. I believe you have what it takes. In time, with the right tools, attitude, and knowledge, you'll have this process covered. You first need to believe in yourself.

Remember, a boxer has to train mentally first and then physically to become 'match fit.' Muhammed Ali, one of the greatest boxers of our time, would often have a psychological edge over his opponents. Many said he would win the fight before he even stepped into the ring because of his mindset and approach. He exuded self-confidence, demonstrated self-belief, and communicated effectively why he was great.

You will do the same, so consider this book as a tool to help you train. You are learning tips to begin your dogged approach to job searching. Conditioning your mind for success. Executing your plan. Communicating your value. Demonstrating your confidence by showing belief in your own abilities. The rest is straightforward.

My aim is to help you stand out from the crowd and get you noticed by the employer. Aiming to get you onto a short-list of candidates selected to attend an interview. Ultimately, helping you to find and secure a position in your chosen occupation, whatever that picture looks like for you. I want you to achieve your career goal whether that is finding a job to pay the bills and get by for now or becoming the next CEO of a huge corporation. It's still a goal, and it's still a process. You just need to build the right strategy and platform for success.

When helping job seekers to build confidence, particularly in their own abilities, I aim to provide a nurturing service along the way. Why? Because I believe that's how you get the best from a person. To be kind. It assists in developing their skills, builds trust and more confidence, eventually propelling a client towards finding employment. More often than not, when clients turn to a Career Coach, it's because they're struggling to find a job or alternative employment on their own and the techniques and 'tools' they are using aren't working. It leaves them feeling frustrated and sometimes exhausted, unsure of where to turn next.

I have drawn many of the tips and insights in this book from scenarios I've come across during my own (illustrious) career. Therefore, I feel it's worth sharing because the details from these examples might help to get you to where you want to be. In part, going some way to demonstrate how changing up the way you think about job searching can create elevated results. Some of them may even make you smile!

In life and at work, I always aim to keep things light, positive and throw in a bit of fun banter along the way. The same applies here. If I can describe strategies and share information in a more engaging and upbeat, vibrant manner, well, then you'll probably have more chance of remembering the details. It's a technique I use regularly in workshops. It appears to be far more interesting listening to someone who loves life, has a positive attitude, is passionate and has a genuine desire to want to help you and keep you engaged.

Whereas listening to someone (me) sounding as boring as 'bat shit' leaves the listener feeling like the exercise was dull and a complete waste of time.

Important notation. Given what I have just explained, please be assured, I am all fully aware the job searching process can be a serious business. I understand and respect it can be a trying process. In some cases, it's about peoples' livelihoods. That's why I aim to help.

Just today I met a lady who was a participant in a workshop and she called me aside. She was in tears because of the lack of progress she was making in her job searching efforts. But after listening to the details I shared, she felt better, armed with knowledge and more enlightened. Therefore, she has hit the 'restart button' and is going to begin again with a fresh approach and re-energise her efforts.

My primary aim is to keep you motivated and help you progress forwards on your job seeking journey. And it is a journey, often with a few ups and downs thrown in for good measure. Some journeys are longer than others too, yet worthwhile when you reach the final destination. Hopefully, you will feel the same by the time you get to the end of the book. Rewarded for taking the time to learn some new techniques and feeling more enlightened, energised, rearing to go and ready to get stuck in.

The examples used in ***Get Your Rear into Gear*** have been drawn from my personal experiences. I've worked in Recruitment Agencies, Human Resources departments, Disability Employment Services (something I'm very proud of), and Job Active – Employment Providers, (helping individuals who receive Centrelink payments to find employment). My Career Coaching clients include Australian Defence Force spouses and partners, face to face and virtual group Career Workshops for government and corporate clients locally, nationally and internationally. I've also worked with Prisoner Employment Programs, Youth Employment Programs, and facilitated Entrepreneurial workshops.

I'm incredibly passionate about what I do and love helping individuals like you to become 'Independent Job Seekers.' It is one of the greatest feelings in the world to hear a workshop participant or one-to-one - client has landed an offer of employment because of the tips, guidance, instructions or information they have picked up during a session.

When first starting, my aim was to emulate the proverb by Chinese philosopher, Confucius.

"*Give a Man a Fish and He will eat for a day. Teach a Man to fish and He will eat for a lifetime.*"

That's the reason behind why I became a Career Coach. To support others, do my research, share insights, help job seekers to achieve their best outcomes in their quest to become more successful. And get to where they want to be in their careers and in life regardless of their circumstances, good or bad. It's also my motivation behind writing this book. To reach as many people as possible on this planet and help 1,000,000+ job seekers to find paid employment.

Business development is another passion of mine. Which has fortunately produced some solid results. I've Coached many clients with start-up businesses for productivity and sales training. Sometimes, you will hear me refer to terms in the book used in business and commerce too, because a number of those strategies can be applied equally effectively during your job searching journey.

I'm also part of the Australian AusMumpreneur Networking Group. A cool group of like-minded women connecting one another to new business opportunities and training. It may be worthwhile checking them out if you're going to start a business or want to turn your side hustle into a more permanent gig as an alternative to finding employment as an employee.

www.ausmumpeneur.com.au

I get zero kickbacks or commission for promoting any services or products in the book. If I believe there is a useful piece of information worth sharing, with the sole purpose of helping you to progress in some way, it'll be in here!

By describing various scenarios I have come across, including the good, the bad and the ugly, I hope will also go some way towards illustrating to you that you're not on your own.

Other job seekers also face similar challenges and situations too, just like the ones you may be facing. The only difference is, for the successful ones, they have now learnt to develop their skills and attitude to become more resolute than ever and succeed regardless of the odds against them. By eventually overcoming hurdles in front of them and driving each to advance their efforts, they speed up the process of securing employment. It's about becoming solution-focused. There is a solution available, you just have to find out what it looks like. Whether that be for a short-term gig or long-term career goal. Whichever one fits your circumstances; I hope you find the examples relatable and beneficial throughout your job searching journey.

Dr. Stephen Hawking (English theoretical physicist, cosmologist, and author and generally clever guy) said:

"In my opinion, there is no aspect of reality beyond the reach of the human mind."

In basic terms, I think this means if you allow yourself to believe something is possible, you will make it a reality. But you first have to believe.

Before you begin, please grab a highlighter pen. I know defacing a book is not in our nature and goes against everything we have been taught. However, yes, you heard me right. Please grab a highlighter pen in readiness to highlight the areas of the book that will resonate with you the most so you can easily find that particular tip or section again.

I created this book as a tool for you to access as often as needed. All tools deserve a little wear and tear to get the job done.

PREFACE

I believe with my whole heart that everyone has the right to hold down a job or find long-term, sustainable employment if they choose. I also believe it's achievable for anyone.

Success might come in the form of a job offer in your profession, chosen occupation, area of expertise, or a traineeship. It may be a promotion, a higher level of professional success you have been dreaming of. Or, it could be a steppingstone job in your career to provide for you and your loved ones. Maybe it's a part-time role, or a voluntary position to gain more experience in readiness to embark on your new career in a different field you have never tried before. Maybe a part-time job whilst you are studying and working towards your longer-term career goals. Whatever the reason for job searching, there is normally a wider vision that we are working towards and aiming for a bigger picture.

Bearing in mind, not all of us know what we want to do when starting out in our careers. I certainly never did! However, after my second paid job as a Recruitment Consultant when I was seventeen, I knew what I wanted to do in the long-term. The joyous feeling of helping someone to find paid employment from an early age has stayed with me forever.

Setting others up on a career path and providing direction to shape careers (regularly changing many lives into the bargain), leaves you with a very triumphant feeling. It is the most gratifying job I could have ever wished for. Fortunately, I seem to have a fairly natural ability to see in others what they can't always see in themselves. Which is a valuable skill as a Career Coach.

Obtaining a satisfying career or rewarding job can give us a higher sense of purpose in life. Paid employment can help us reach our personal and professional goals. Which creates a higher level of personal fulfilment, giving us a greater sense of self-esteem and brings about many additional benefits.

Some of those benefits can include:

- A clear sense of direction.
- Personal contentment.
- Financial gains.
- Social benefits.
- Rewarding careers lasting a lifetime.
- A greater sense of self-worth.
- Increased levels of confidence.
- Independence.
- A greater sense of identity.
- Work-life balance.
- New skills.
- Meeting new people.

Gaining employment, finding a job we love or establishing a long-term career, often helps us to enjoy life to the fullest.

Sir William Booth, founder of The Salvation Army wrote a book about the plight of the poor in England called ***'In Darkest England and the Way Out.'*** In it, he outlined a programme to help the poor and needy, something he termed ***'The Cab Horse Charter,'*** claiming that in England, cab horses were better cared for than millions of the poorest people.

In the East End of London, in 1865 a cab horse had a purpose. To pull a cab or load.

- If it was weary, someone helped it to its feet.
- If it was hungry, someone gave it food.
- Thirsty, given water.
- Tired, time to rest.
- Above all, it had a job.
- A purpose in life and a place in society.

The owners treated the horse with a higher level of respect than millions of poor people in those days.

Sir William Booth had a vision, and he wanted people to have the same rights as the cab horse, which was a sense of purpose and personal fulfilment. Self-respect and dignity.

His vision was similar to the vision of John Bird and Gordon Roddick, the founders of ***The Big Issue*** magazine founded in 1991. It was a response to the increasing numbers of homeless people in London, some of whom they'd been friends with for many years. The Big Issue is a non-for-profit social enterprise that develops solutions to help homeless, marginalised and disadvantaged people positively change their lives and circumstances. In 2016, The Big Issue celebrated surpassing 200 million magazine sales.

When a person has a sense of purpose, such as having a job to sell a magazine, it enables them to contribute to society and helps to restore dignity. Provides a sense of purpose and rebuilds pride.

Both plights have resonated with me because I hope, and pray, particularly now at a time of high unemployment, that all job seekers regardless of their current circumstances can find a job and be given the chance to improve their personal circumstances - if that's what they choose.

During times of high unemployment, especially for those who have lost a job or been made redundant because of cutbacks and the economic downturn, it's very easy to lose self-motivation, dignity and self-belief.

But I'm here to tell you there are opportunities out there. Australia is a land of great natural resources, but more often than not we have to dig for the gold. It is the same with job searching.

A great quote by the American motivational speaker Les Brown:

"To be successful, you must be willing to do the things today others won't do in order to have the things tomorrow others won't have."

That's why I wrote ***Get Your Rear into Gear.*** A motivational, practical, self-help book, crammed with information, tips and above all knowledge to help people just like you, from all walks of life, of any age, to accomplish a greater level of success when searching for a job.

Whether you are a:

- Mum re-entering the workforce after starting a family.
- School leaver unsure of where or how to start looking for employment.
- Mature aged job seeker needing direction to identify your transferrable skills or consider alternative career paths.
- A graduate who wants to learn how to approach an employer in the first instance, unsure of which details to include on the application.
- A job seeker just needing to understand the essential ingredients of what an effective resume should contain.
- A Tradie needing some insights on where to find success or

how to start job searching in today's job market.
- A person of professional standing just needing to build or rebuild your confidence.

This book is written for you all—the job seekers from a wide section of the community. Because the principals remain the same. It is a process. And to achieve true success, we need to get crystal clear on the outcome before we begin. Establish our 'end-game'. Focus on the final result before setting out on the journey in the first place.

Sometimes, we all need a little help to ***'Get our Rear Into Gear.'***

Remember, you're the Boxer and I am your Corner Man. You are in the ring, fighting the fight. But I am in the corner ready to help. I aim to give you the guidance, to keep motivated and go the distance. Throwing in tips on how to beat your competition.

So, if you have been made redundant, are currently unemployed, need a change of direction, or need a little help getting your job searching journey back on track, I'm here to tell you, there has never been a better time to pursue those employment goals, and put your best foot forward now. You are a worthy candidate.

Many of us procrastinate because we want to protect ourselves from feelings of stress or discomfort. We become less motivated because of the fear of rejection. None of us like to be told we have been unsuccessful in any area of our life. Especially when it comes to being declined for that job we really wanted!

But once we treat everything as a process where you have everything to gain and nothing to lose, you will see progress and gravitate towards finding success.

Often, we can hold ourselves back or self-sabotage because we think it's better to not apply for that job, ultimately never learning if we might have succeeded. Rather than applying and learning we have been unsuccessful, and getting our feelings hurt into the bargain. But that solution is only a state of mind. It's the mindset that we have to change first. We have to push ourselves out of our comfort zones to grow. Whilst it may feel a little uncomfortable to begin with, the process gets easier in time.

Let's partner up throughout this career journey - together and see where it takes us. Aim to achieve success and positive results. Expect to be successful and you probably will be!

Tip 1

GET YOUR REAR INTO GEAR

- N.O.W. Meaning: No Opportunity Wasted.
- It's time to get cracking today!
- Stop procrastinating, and just do it!
- Let's not put off until tomorrow what can be done today.

As a mum, I'm regularly telling my three little boys to 'Get a Wriggle on,' meaning, 'Hurry Up' or 'Get a Move on.' The expression of ***Get Your Rear into Gear*** is communicated with the same level of affection. But make no mistake, there is no time like the present to contact employers and get a move on. It's vital you start your job searching strategy with a sense of urgency.

In 1935, the great English poet, Geoffrey Chaucer, used this phrase in the prologue of '*The Clerk's Tale*' from his *Canterbury Tales* collection. "*Time and Tide wait for no man!*"

Otherwise, how else will an employer know you're out there looking for a job? They won't come to you unless you tell them you're available, and ready to go. From this moment forward, you are in charge of your own destiny. As the saying goes, 'you have to be in it to win it!' Right now, we are in this together. I'm on your side. I'm going to help guide you towards achieving your desired outcomes with a little 'Momma B' encouragement thrown in to keep you on track.

We are all guilty of putting tasks off until the very last minute because we prefer not to spend energy on the things that give us little pleasure or frankly, we can't be bothered. Or, we are trying to protect ourselves from feelings like stress, anxiety, or failure.

If we're not good at something, we are less likely to either try it or throw ourselves into it 'hook, line and sinker.' We assume we might fail, therefore don't even attempt the task in the first place. However, now the time has come to start getting on with things. Pronto!

Procrastination is a thing of the past. If you want to show an employer your true grit, and demonstrate you have what it takes to be a great employee, stand out from the crowd and set yourself apart from your competition. Now is the time to prove your worth.

Begin with 'having a little word with yourself.' Even tell yourself, "I have what it takes to conquer my fears." Push yourself out of your comfort zone. Apply a different approach to the one you have used in the past, try something new. But make sure you put your best foot forward A.S.A.P.

Nothing needs to hold you back. Get off your bum today! If you choose not to, then please understand this: The current job market is only going to get tougher because of the economic climate after Covid-19. Which means in the coming weeks and months it might become harder to secure employment, harder than ever before, or since the last big recession in the early 1990s.

Having lost my own job in Recruitment because of a recession in 1991, I fully understand what a bleak employment market looks like. So it's imperative you have everything organised and in order in readiness to progress with your job applications as quickly as possible.

I've known some job application processes to take anywhere between three and six months, depending on the role. (Security clearances can take months, especially if you have migrated to a new country). Try to keep in mind a sense of urgency.

The good news is, if you are prepared and know where to look for jobs and understand the value you're offering an employer; it will make it easier to secure work and you'll progress much faster. It's better to think about changing your circumstances sooner rather than later. Even if you are not ready to move yet, start building your platform for success now so you are prepared for when it is the right time to do so.

- Begin making the relevant connections with employers on LinkedIn and build networks.
- Sort out your foundation documentation, be prepared and become organised.
- Get on with the research.
- Establish everything you need to know about the qualifications your ideal employer expects.
- Embark on further professional development.
- Become a lifelong learner.
- Think about your skills, experience, qualifications, strengths and begin to draft your elevator pitch (more on 'elevator pitch' in Resume section).
- Build your networks.
- Create a 'template email' to send to friends, family, old colleagues. Explain you're available for new opportunities. Ask them if they could get back to you with any leads or referrals to employers.

Once you have undertaken the steps needed to get ahead, you will then feel more confident about approaching employers with the purpose of sharing your credentials. Inevitably feeling more comfortable about communicating your true worth.

- Start immediately with a sense of urgency.
- Let's go.
- Let's start today!
- Let's start immediately.

Remember the Boxer example? Do you think they would be sitting eating pies right now in preparation for the upcoming match to beat their competitor? Or doing sit-ups, scrunches, squats, skipping, running, shadow boxing and sparring? The Boxer will be training the brain to become mentally and physically fit. It's a well-known fact that athletes visualise their success over and over again before undertaking the action.

You are replicating what other professionals do. You are creating habits for success. Training your mind, implementing new techniques to get you to where you want to be.

This is your chance to become mentally prepared and progress to success.

Here's a famous quote by Martin Luther King Jr., the famous American Civil Rights Leader.

"Take the first step in faith. You don't have to see the whole staircase, just take the first step."

Just start with one easy step because that's all it will take to experience a sense of accomplishment, setting yourself up on the path to progress.

Tip 2

PROOFREAD, PROOFREAD, AND PROOFREAD AGAIN!

If this book was only two pages in length, and I needed to choose one critical tip throughout the whole job searching process and more likely to bring forward a higher chance of success, it would be this.

Proofread, proofread, and proofread again!

It is vital you ask someone to **proofread your resume, job applications and cover letter** before sending out your details to any prospective employer. Choose someone who you feel would be good in this area. Teachers are usually helpful and knowledgeable. Consider librarians, or a local Career Advisor, many of whom are free to use if they are available via a government service. Otherwise, a friend or parent or friend's parent who has a decent command of the English language. Basically, someone who can pick up or point out any errors that need correcting—before you send it!

There is a saying. *"Can't see the wood for the trees."*

It means you are so involved and concerned with all the small details (the trees) of a situation, you're almost unable to get a clear overview of the whole situation (the wood) and so lose any real perspective. It's the same with your resume. If you have written it and read it half a dozen times, then you are more likely to miss the typos because you are too close to it now. Having read it so many times before, the information becomes blended.

Spell check on computers are great; however, spell check only corrects words that are spelt incorrectly. Therefore, if you use a word in the wrong context but it is spelt correctly, the spell checker will not always pick it up.

Another example is when spell check does not highlight errors that have been written in block capital letters. I have seen it happen loads of times on resumes.

I can't impress this point enough. You must get someone to check your documentation for typos or spelling errors **before** you send it out. It is a vital part of job searching and one that can help you progress quickly, or have your application declined rapidly too.

Employers decline way too many job applications based on simple mistakes. This is one of the main reasons a person's job application is unsuccessful. It is littered with errors. End of story.

When working with clients every day, I get the chance to see job applications, resumes, LinkedIn profiles and cover letters. Sometimes written by so called 'professionals,' they still have errors. It drives me crackers!

These job seekers are amazing people aiming to find employment. Qualified, experienced, outgoing, skilled, professional, level-headed, calm, diligent, etc. But they're telling me they're not experiencing any degree of success finding a job. Or they don't seem to obtain any kind of traction with their job applications. Sometimes, never hearing back from an employer (this happens regularly these days, which can be mega-frustrating).

When I start working with a person, I can determine almost immediately why their applications have been unsuccessful so far. Nine times out of ten, it's these tiny things that make a big difference.

Let me give you an example of something that happened a few weeks ago when I met a degree-holding, qualified Human Resources professional for the first time. It took me around twenty seconds to pick up three typos on the first page of her resume. She wondered why she was being declined for job opportunities.

This is not an example of me trying to embarrass anyone (clearly not using anyone's name here). This is purely an example of a person who was pressed for time when writing her resume. She explained she did not have time to ask anyone to proofread her documentation. This lady spent four years obtaining a degree. That's a lot of work. Given the fact she was also studying HR, tells me she is a bright person with a good work ethic.

Regardless of how qualified you are for a job, there is never any excuse to have your resume let you down. Especially when it comes to simple spelling mistakes.

Once, I declined an internal applicant for a senior level role because he spelt his own name incorrectly on his resume. True story!

At first, I thought it was laughable. But then, after getting over the initial shock, I had to seriously consider whether the lack of attention applied to his application would overspill into a work-related situation. To be fair, how can you expect any hiring manager to consider your application if you can't even spell your own name correctly. I know it was a simple typo. But when you have thirty other applicants equally qualified, knowledgeable and experienced applicants to review, you must make a decision based on the information set out in front of you. I had no choice but to decline his application. I provided him gentle feedback though, so he could put it right next time. He was understanding and grateful. Who knows how many other job offers he may have otherwise lost out on.

The reason I share these details is because it happens way too often. Needless to say, this is the biggest reason employers decline most job applications. Yes, I know I am hammering home the point. But it's a point worth hammering.

I conducted a survey of over fifty employers when I started my business. I asked the Recruitment person, Hiring Manager or Business Owner what were the contributing factors for declining a job seeker's application. The overwhelming evidence, and number one key factor—errors in the resume or job application.

If you are aiming to make a great first impression, and there are typos throughout your documentation, what faith will an employer have in your ability to pay high attention to detail to their business? Whether it be in the office, on site, in a healthcare department or on the road, they won't hire you.

High attention to detail means checking the small stuff. In some roles, it's a critical part of the responsibilities. Think Accounts Payable roles. What happens if you enter an additional zero when paying a supplier. It can make the difference between paying someone $1,000 or $10,000. That's nine grand's worth of mistake! Too much for any employer to handle. Whilst it might seem insignificant to some, it isn't. Especially to a Hiring Manager.

In a crowded job market, employers are almost looking for a reason to decline your application. Because there are so many good job seekers looking for work. Having typos in either a cover letter or resume makes it easy for a HR person or the Hiring Manager to make a negative decision based on the details you have provided. They have almost no choice but to decline your details.

For now, at least, if you read nothing else in this book, go back to your resume and cover letter and get someone to proofread it immediately. Someone you trust.

This book aims to show you how to help a Hiring Manager make a positive decision regarding your job application, providing them with a persuasive argument set out in your:

- Cover Letter.
- Resume.
- LinkedIn profile.

Get Your Rear into Gear has been created for you, the job seeker, who wants to improve your chances of success in today's job market. I hope you find at least some of the guidance, tips, and examples helpful to propel you towards success.

Tip 3

START WITH A SPIRIT OF OPTIMISM

The first step to finding lasting employment is crucial for you to understand if you are to secure any chance of real success. This is the number one golden rule you must apply to help you progress and eventually succeed. Start with a spirit of optimism! Begin with a positive attitude and a wholehearted expectation of achieving the desired results you're aiming for. In other words: Believe in yourself!

This essential attitude will help to maintain your levels of motivation to attain the job you are ultimately seeking. I'm not saying it will happen the first time every time. But, if you can start to believe it will happen, then your positive attitude will gain momentum, and often carry you over the finish line. Persuading an employer to believe in you becomes a whole lot easier when you believe in yourself first.

To accomplish any degree of achievement, whether it's on a short, medium or long-term basis, job searching or otherwise, your motivation needs to be kept at an optimum level to create the outcome you are hoping for. Otherwise you could quickly fall flat on your face. That's not what we want to happen here.

If we begin with the expectation of success, and do not waiver in our levels of optimism, success will happen. I have seen time and time again the enhanced results job seekers and clients have achieved when they have started out the process with a positive attitude. It makes a world of difference!

I have also experienced the negative results of what can happen when a job seeker sets out with a poor attitude, inevitably receiving negative results.

There is a famous saying.

"Attitude is everything – so make sure you pick a good one!"

By starting with an optimistic approach from the very beginning, you're setting yourself up for a positive experience. Beginning with an expectation of accomplishing quality results and doing everything in your power to achieve those results, will gravitate you towards attaining the goal. When you believe in yourself and in your own abilities (because you are communicating your worth with an increased level of passion, enthusiasm and optimism), an employer will feel the same way. Then it's more likely the employer will 'buy into you.'

Tip 4

BUILD YOUR EMPLOYER WISH LIST - WHO AND WHY

What is an 'Employer Wish List' and why build one?

It's really important for you to understand this part of the job-hunting process. Once you know WHO you want to work for and WHY you want to work there, it will provide you with a clearer sense of direction in terms of your end goal.

Plus, there'll be a much stronger likelihood of getting offered a job by that particular employer. Why? Because you will have done your homework and figured out exactly what these kinds of employers are looking for from prospective employees. You will understand their expectations as an employer, and you can meet their needs by stating your case (communicating effectively by building a stronger case in your resume, job application and interview). This demonstrates to an employer you have what it takes to fit the requirements of the job and why you are a great match for the company.

Effectively, you will be happy to receive an offer of employment and satisfied with the job in the long run, increasing the likelihood of staying in the role for the longer-term.

Figure out which employers you want to target first. They're the companies who will likely be looking for employees just like you, the applicant who matches their expectations and needs to fulfil the requirements of the role.

If, when starting out, you take a 'Willy-nilly' approach, (yes, a professional term I use regularly), stabbing in the dark and hoping for the best, you are setting yourself up for limited or poor results. Putting it bluntly, that approach just ain't going to fly!

It will be a waste of your time, effort and energy. Like throwing a handful of mud at a wall and hoping some of it sticks. Why not perfect your aim and choose a more impressive wall where the mud will stick time and time again?

Job searching is just like any other search. It is more likely to be successful if it is planned and well-organised from the beginning. If you are searching for something, you need to know what you're looking for, where you need to look to find it, and how you are going to apply your efforts to find it. Being organised and starting your job searching early will pay dividends later, potentially setting you up for success in both your career and personal life.

Creating an Employer Wish List is choosing to take a proactive approach.

REMEMBER, when you're not employed, and you want to be, it's your full-time job to find a job no matter how long it takes.

Ask yourself, "Do I really want to make this happen?" If the answer is yes, then build your platform for success right now.

What to put on your Employer Wish List? Bearing in mind, you might not even know anything about the companies you want to work with yet. You may have recently relocated and know nothing about the area. You may have never had a job before. But don't worry about that. It will all fall into place.

I call it the filter process. Imagine a bucket. Start putting ideas in the top and then start filtering out information as you need to. Discard the irrelevant employers you find do not meet your criteria for employment based on what works for you. Then, what you're left with (at the bottom) gives you a clearer idea of who and where you want to work.

Points you may want to take into consideration when building your Employer Wish List.

- Company, nature of business. What does the organisation do? Does it align with my values?
- Industry type – examples: Retail, Hospitality, Healthcare, Community, Finance, Mining/Oil/Gas, Construction, Professional Services, Non-for-profit, Government.
- Performance of the business?
- Annual turnover?
- Benefits?
- Will it be able to provide a good salary level?
- Commission/Bonus structure?
- Healthcare?
- Company vehicle?
- Rewards and recognition?
- Good reputation?
- Size/Number of employees:
  - › 1-19 Employees = Small.
  - › 20-250 Employees = SME (SME means Small to Medium Enterprise).
  - › Large 250+ Employees.
- Corporate?
- International?
- Global?

- Locations: Local, National, Multi-national.
- Logistics: Travel time?
- How to get there?
  - › Public Transport.
  - › Walk.
  - › Drive/Car Share.
  - › Relocate.
  - › FIFO – Fly in Fly Out.
  - › DIDO – Drive in Drive Out.
- Type of employment?
  - › Part-time.
  - › Full-time.
  - › Permanent.
  - › Casual.
  - › Contract.
  - › Temporary.
  - › Freelance.
  - › Self-Employed.
  - › Flexible Working Arrangements.
  - › Work from home.
  - › Virtual.
  - › Family oriented.
  - › Job Share.
  - › Flexible hours.
- Opportunity for career progression?
- Work experience.
- Apprenticeship.
- Traineeship.
- Internship.
- Grad Scheme.
- Training and Development budget?

A team at the University of Oxford's Saïd Business School has produced evidence of what many people have long suspected. **Happier people do a better job.**

Its six-month study of 1,800 call centre workers at British telecom firm BT, found a clear, causal effect of happiness on productivity. They asked the workers to rate their happiness each week via an email survey comprising of five emoji buttons, from very sad to very happy.

Interestingly, the happy staff did not put in more hours than their unhappy colleagues to achieve their superior results. They just used their time more productively.

Previous studies have shown paid work ranks low in most people's idea of happiness, and employers generally need to make a bigger effort to ensure employees are content in their jobs. That's according to Professor Jan-Emmanuel De Neve, one of the authors of the Saïd Business School report.

"There seems to be considerable room for improvement in the happiness of employees while they are at work," he has noted. "While this is clearly in the interest of workers themselves, our analysis suggests it is also in the interests of their employers."

Happy employees not only worked faster, making more calls per hour, but also achieved 13% higher sales than their unhappy colleagues.

Another example is from Sir Richard Branson, Virgin billionaire tycoon. Branson himself famously said:

"Take care of your employees and they'll take care of everything else."

Bearing in mind he has a net worth of around $5 billion, it's hard to argue with him.

The overall point being this; good employers look after their employees. Which for you means you really want to find a good employer by having done a little research and then sticking them on your Employer Wish List. You may have already heard of the term 'employer of choice.' Below is a brief explanation of why it's helpful for you to consider identifying who could be a better employer to work for.

An employer of choice:

- A business that has worked hard to ensure the employees are happy and productive because research has proven that happier employers are more productive employees.
- Disgruntled employees regularly have a much higher rate of absenteeism and lower productivity levels in the workplace.
- Good employers understand that happy employees feel more settled at work and are prepared to do what it takes to get the job done. A happy employee feels valued by their manager and chooses to go the 'extra mile' because they understand eventually their efforts will be valued, recognised and rewarded.
- Larger organisations understand the need to retain good employees. Above all, it's a great cost saving exercise.
- Staff recruitment is a huge cost to any business, especially if the employee leaves after a short while and the process has to begin again.
- Human Resources departments across the world understand this concept. As a result, many employers of choice today have implemented new departments dedicated to growing a more engaged workforce. Many larger businesses with a HR department will have a person or a team of staff dedicated to 'People and Culture.'

- What's the purpose of the People and Culture Department? To lead the development and implementation of the organisation's employee and engagement approach and drive initiatives to improve the overall organisational performance and culture for everyone in the business.

In short, happier, engaged employees stay longer and get more done. Target employers with a good reputation. It will save you having to look for another job in a few months.

So, now we have identified what an employer of choice is. Please understand, not all employers are alike and employers of choice. I hope this leaves you feeling somewhat clearer on who you're going to be approaching for a job.

Next stop… Identifying your Non-Negotiable list.

Tip 5

IDENTIFY YOUR NON-NEGOTIABLE LIST

We all have a list of our own non-negotiables when it comes to accepting or declining a job offer. It is better to be aware of what yours looks like to help you make a more decisive decision regarding where to work right from the start. Your non-negotiables follow your values and principles and define not only what you will and won't accept from others, but also what you will and won't accept from yourself. They are the big-time deal breakers.

The flip side of not knowing what your non-negotiables are could be accepting a role and then having to leave because you hadn't taken some critical stuff into account. Here is an example list to help you build your own list.

- Pay – How much do you need to earn?
- Pay – How much would you really like to earn?
- Pay – Cycle; weekly, fortnightly, monthly?
- Location of workplace. How far are you willing to travel?
- How much will it cost you to get to work?
- Which hours are you prepared to work?

- Part-time, full-time, weekends, evenings, shifts?
- Work conditions? Office, site work, physical, hot, cold, smelly, clean?
- Ethical employer?
- Company culture? What are your expectations?
- Does the employer align with your personal values?
- Family friendly?
- Permanent employment?
- Job security?
- Casual work?
- Nine day fortnight?
- Positive work-life balance?
- Acceptable duties versus unacceptable duties?
- Contract of employment?
- Is there an EBA (Enterprise Bargaining Agreement)?
- What are you willing to do in return for your pay cheque?
- What are you not willing to do?
- Are you prepared to put the kids into day-care?
- Are you prepared to put the kids into before/after school care?

Everyone's non-negotiables are different and personal to them. But it is vital you know what you are willing to do to be paid. Or maybe, more importantly, what you are not willing to do.

Then, when you have approached all the companies on your Employer Wish List, and they meet your criteria, and fit in with your non-negotiables, you are setting yourself up for a more fulfilling employment experience.

Some job seekers I have met have been offered a job, started it, and then left within a short space of time because the company (or job) did not live up to expectations. It was not necessarily the employer's fault. The job seeker didn't consider how long it would take to travel to work. Or whether they could afford to work for that particular rate of pay, after putting the kids into before and after school care, or prior to accepting the job. Some didn't realise they couldn't live on the wages they'd been offered because they were unaware of all of their outgoings. So, they left the job.

Several didn't take into account the negative effects that endless hours of travel time would have on themselves or their family. Travelling up to three hours a day is tough for anyone. Especially if you hadn't given any thought to the long distance up front.

In my early career, I helped a young man to find a job in a warehouse. The role involved shift work. Unfortunately, it turned out that he couldn't stay awake during his first week of nights. His supervisor continually found him napping at every given opportunity. In the toilets, in the breakroom, lying on racking in the warehouse. You'll be forgiven for smiling. Even I chuckled at that one. Especially when his supervisor contacted me to tell me not to send any more temps like 'Snoozy.' Think about the sleepy one from the Seven Dwarfs.

In other examples, I have met job seekers who are prepared to do anything to secure employment. They have travelled far and wide, worked all sorts of hours, tolerated filthy working conditions, across challenging shift patterns. One even relocated to the other side of the country without his family so he could send money home. During hard times, some job seekers recognise it doesn't matter how you make money (I'm talking legally, of course). It can all be spent the same.

We all have non-negotiables. You too will have yours. Establish what they are first, so you can avoid any misunderstanding at the time of receiving a job offer, or even after starting a new job.

Tip 6

COLLATE YOUR FOUNDATION DOCUMENTS

Getting your foundation documents together is key to any successful job searching strategy.

Many job seekers are sadly declined for job opportunities based on not having the right information available, or something is missing from their application, not included in their resume or in the cover letter.

I collectively call these things your foundation documents. Think about your foundation documents in the same way we would if you were building a house. One of the first things a builder needs to do to ensure they lay the foundations of a building correctly, so the timber frame holding the structure together is strong and remains upright at all times. The building has to be strong enough to withstand wind, rain, hail, etc. Therefore, the building ultimately stands the test of time. Without having laid the solid foundations in the first place, the building will fall over, probably sooner rather than later.

Your foundation documents serve you in a similar way. They are the basis to build your future career success. You need to immediately get the documents together in your 'toolbox', (albeit an invisible one). This ensures you have everything ready at your fingertips to give to an employer straight away.

The first three critical items you need to build your platform for success are:

- Resume(s).
- Cover Letter(s).
- Basic LinkedIn profile.

Being prepared is about making sure you have all of your foundation documents ready to go in the early stages of the job searching process. Rather than scrambling around for the all-important details at the last minute, trying to find everything you need when your back is against the wall because of time pressures.

Appearing to be organised, professional, proactive, and motivated gives a great first impression to any employer, even if you don't feel it. *'Actions speak louder than words'* as the saying goes. Showing an employer you have your 'S**t together' speaks volumes.

When you have prepared in advanced, you will give the impression you're more efficient and ultimately more appealing during the hiring process. Who doesn't love a motivated employee who wreaks of efficiency?

A Recruiter *knows* when you have **'Got Your Rear into Gear.'**

In particular, at the interview stage, a HR person upon greeting you will form a quick first opinion. When you arrive early, look the part, turn up ready to discuss a job opportunity with all the necessary documentation available to make the Hiring Manager's job easy, it's an impactful demonstration of your enthusiasm for the job. You are showing the employer why they should pick you—without having said a word. Now that's a great performance in anyone's book.

One of my clients recently attended an interview. She brought everything with her, ready and prepared without having been asked by the employer to do so. She walked out feeling confident about a job offer because she set the stage for a great first impression. They liked her right from the start. She was being interviewed for a Tender Administrator role, a job that requires an efficient approach. She was the only candidate that turned up prepared. Guess what? She was offered a position later that week and started the following week. This young woman was a mum re-entering the workforce. It was a part-time role where she could work from home on a 'virtual' basis one day a week. Perfect to meet her needs.

When an applicant turns up late, looks dishevelled or seems ill-prepared, the HR person also forms an immediate opinion. And it's not always a good one. Which clearly makes the difference between getting a job offer or not.

Take the pressure off yourself and get organised as quickly as possible. Then you will avoid putting yourself under extra pressure during the final stages.

There is nothing worse than seeing a job seeker losing out on that all-important job offer because they didn't have their paperwork (foundation documents) organised well in advance.

Here's an example of some additional details an employer might ask you to provide during an online job application or on the day of an interview:

- Qualifications.
- Certificates.
- Licences.
- Registrations.
- Membership information.
- Police Clearance.

- Working with Children Check.
- 100 points of ID/ 10 years' worth of addresses.
- Work permits or Visa information.
- Residency status details or Citizenship certificates.

When you get asked for foundation documents, always provide a copy and not the original.

Here's an example of what happened early in my career when I was ill-prepared.

I remember assisting a job seeker who wanted to work on a mine site. This young man was on my caseload, and it was my job to help him find a job. I helped him by submitting an application on his behalf to an employer who was advertising a Utilities Worker vacancy for a FIFO position, (Fly In, Fly Out).

The job seeker assured me he possessed everything the employer needed for the job and more. Clean Police record, clean bill of health, full WA driver's licence—all the requirements of the job. I foolishly did not check every tiny detail of the job seeker's foundation documentation prior to submitting his application. Mainly because I felt so confident when I was communicating with him, I didn't think it necessary to double-check everything. Wrong!

The Recruiter was not pleased when they followed up with me the following week after assessing his application. The Recruiter explained they felt as though I'd wasted their time. When I enquired why the candidate wasn't suitable, sounding a little shocked, and not initially understanding why, I discovered I hadn't double-checked the job seeker's driver's licence properly. It turned out he did not have a full manual driver's licence. He only held a licence for an automatic vehicle. I was gutted and unhappy! However, I only had myself to blame because I did not check the fine details. I took the young man's word for it that he had everything necessary to undertake the job.

Had he not been so self-assured, I don't think I would have been.

Basically, when you go to a mine site, more often than not, the vehicles used on sites are vehicles with a manual gearbox. Which means you have to have a full manual licence to drive one, and you can't when you have only passed a driving test in an automatic vehicle. It requires a different test completely.

Be assured, that only happened once. It cost me a lot of time trying to rebuild my reputation and mend the relationship with the Recruitment Team. Afterwards, the job seeker received a verbal kick up the bum from me too because he had not been entirely honest about which licence he was legally permitted to use.

It can happen to all of us. Had I arranged the job seeker's foundation documents in advance, I would have left myself enough time to have checked whether he had the correct licence to do the job.

Notation regarding LinkedIn, please remember, even though a LinkedIn profile is not normally described as a document, I wanted to make sure it is included on the list. An up-to-date LinkedIn profile available for an employer to review, learn more about you and see a photo of you, is a key component when thinking about your tools for success. More about LinkedIn later on Tip 41.

I can't overstate the importance of being organised with your foundation documents right from the outset. To succeed, and beat your competitors in an employer-driven market, they require you to stand out from the crowd. Therefore, have everything proofread, verified and double-checked ready for submission when an opportunity arises.

Tip 7

CONDUCT RESEARCH BEFORE PREPARING YOUR RESUME

Even before you build a resume, you must conduct some **thorough research** into the roles and employers you will approach with it.

It is essential you understand exactly **who you are targeting**, and the skillset they are looking for. Whether you are creating a resume for a job hunt or an expression of interest, you need to identify the most sought-after skills and experience for the positions you are hoping to land. Otherwise you will simply be using guesswork to populate your resume.

Browse through the websites of companies on your '**wish list**' and businesses you would like to work for. Read through their 'About Us' page. This will provide you with vital clues regarding:

- Size of the company.
- Structure.
- Nature of Business.
- Company growth.
- Types of projects.
- Where they operate.

- Who are their customers?
- Company strategy.
- News articles.
- Core values.
- Organisation or strategic vision.
- Other opportunities from this employer.
- Leadership team.
- Purpose or vision.
- Mission statement.
- Health and Safety performance.

Find out what they are looking for in their employees, then weave this terminology into your documentation. Then it's ready for the employer to see you are the employee who 'mirrors' their values and meets the needs of their vision for their future business growth. Ask yourself some test questions. Why is this employer in business? To make money and be more productive? To address climate change? To develop something? Solve a problem?

The main point of this exercise is twofold.

1. To show your prospective employer you have taken the time to understand their needs, and you have completed preparation to prove you have what it takes to be a great employee.
2. To outshine your competitors on the day of the interview, knocking the socks off the interviewer or hiring manager, demonstrating your interest and enthusiasm for what they do. To the point that they only have one clear winner to choose from. That'll be you!

Tip 8

HAVE MULTIPLE RESUMES

Often, I get asked, "Can I have more than one resume?" Yes, you can.

Remember, you are still being honest with the overall content (no little 'porky pies' please). It means we can write it with a different slant depending on the job you are applying for.

You can have an 'Admin resume' and a 'Sales resume' because you have undertaken both roles previously and some duties overlap. As a consideration, focus on Admin key responsibilities when you are applying for Admin jobs. That's because the employer will then assess your suitability based on the key responsibility details you have provided as an Admin person. Ideally, it will leave them concluding you have the relevant experience to undertake the responsibilities of the job.

If the Career History part of your resume indicates you have no experience in the field they are looking for, it's unlikely an employer will select your resume for short-listing. Especially if you have nothing to match what is outlined in the advert.

The bonus bit of having multiple resumes means you can apply for different jobs simultaneously without having to painstakingly rewrite your resume again and again.

Be sure to tweak the key skills required for the particular occupation being advertised, keeping in mind what the employer is seeking and aim to match their needs. Still do your homework about the company too! For example:

- A Business Development resume might focus on increased sales, territory management and sales results.
- A Recruitment resume could highlight relationship management, networking, value of candidate placements, and the diverse range of talent pools managed.
- An Admin resume might focus on efficiencies, office systems implemented, money saved by combining suppliers, time saved by remedying administrative issues.

Whichever number of resumes you build, remember, your resume has to be achievement focused. Think Awards, recognition, industry training.

Tip 9

BUILD A WINNING RESUME

This tip, and all of the resume tips including Tip 35 on page 111 are dedicated to writing a winning resume. I feel they are all worth dwelling on for a while because it's an area where many people still require assistance. I have tried to demystify what is required from a great resume.

A great resume is the single most important 'tool' in your job searching armoury.

What is a Resume?

- A resume is a document that summarises your **work experience, education, skills and achievements** for a prospective employer and outlines your accomplishments in relation to the role you are aiming to land.
- It is usually required as part of a job application and is considered essential information for an employer to assess whether an applicant is a suitable candidate for an interview.
- A resume is an effective marketing tool to sell yourself when approaching potential employers. You should think

of your resume as a billboard to advertise why you're a great candidate for the position.

- A resume is also required when you are submitting an expression of interest for a potential role or creating a 'Career Profile' directly with an organisation or when setting up 'Job Alerts.'

What should you include in your Resume?

- What you include on your resume has only a few moments to capture the interest of a potential employer. Your message must be clear and concise, enticing and relevant. But above all else, it has to be easy for a Recruiter or a Hiring Manager to read**. Think clean and crisp, not too cluttered.**
- Research shows on average it takes a Recruiter between 6-30 seconds to read your resume and make a decision. Yep! That's enough to make you cry into your wine or beer glass. Now you understand why it's so important to get your resume looking 'Tip Top.'
- A winning resume is **achievement-focused**, beautifully formatted, keyword optimised matching the selection criteria, grammatically correct and… more!

Tip 10

RESUME HEADER - ESSENTIAL INGREDIENTS

- **Heading** – The heading should be at the top of the document, either centred or placed to the right. Your name should be in bold and the biggest font on the page. You want an employer to remember your name.
- **Name – First and Last name(s):** Your first and last name is sufficient on a resume. Write your name how you like to be addressed at work. It can become confusing if you write your legal name, but you are known as something completely different. At the interview stage, you can explain the difference. Keep things as simple as possible. If your legal name differs from your usual name, use the name you want to be addressed by. Try to keep it as effortless as possible for a Hiring Manager to address you correctly and without causing unnecessary confusion.
- **Home Address** – It is not necessary to include your full postal address. A suburb is sufficient. You do not have to include your suburb either if you don't want to. Remember, some employers may take into account the

distance you are travelling and the time it would take you to get to and from work. In some instances, employers have declined job applicants because they have deemed it too far for the person to travel and assumed the individual would probably leave after a short time.

- **Telephone/Mobile contact number** – Ensure contact details are accurate and up to date. If you have changed your mobile number, make sure it has been amended on the resume. It could make the difference between receiving a call from an employer – or not! Choose one contact number, not several.
- **Email address** – Only include a regular or professional email address. Create a new one if necessary. Do not include an inappropriate email address. Do not use your current work email address on your personal resume either. It comes across as sloppy. Applications can be declined based on an email address, especially if it's entirely inappropriate. Be a good representative for the organisation you're applying to. Consider this: It's great to have a sense of humour but save it for social circles.
- Include your **LinkedIn URL** as this is a great way to catch the attention of a Hiring Manager. It entices an employer to look at your LinkedIn profile and learn more about you. An employer will get to see your photo and hopefully connect with you. If an employer likes what they see on your resume and LinkedIn profile, they are more likely to invite you for an interview.
- Add a link to your webpage: **www.alisonbannister.com** if it is relevant to the role you are applying for. Adding a www. is a great way for an employer to learn more about you if you already have a business or project available for

them to see. If you are in website design and you have created several websites, this would be a good place to share your portfolio.

- **Date of birth** – It is not necessary to include your date of birth. But some jobs require you to be eighteen or over by law. So, it is an expectation you would provide it.
- **Marital Status** – No need to include your marital status. It's your choice.

Tip 11

BUILD AN ENTICING ELEVATOR PITCH

What is an 'Elevator Pitch?' This is a one paragraph description (three to four sentences) explaining why you are the best person for the job.

It can be called Professional Profile, Career Summary or some call it Career Objective. I call it Professional Profile.

Introduce yourself. The first thing a Recruiter or Hiring Manager wants to know when reading your resume and seeing your 'Elevator Pitch' is:

- **Who you are?** Communicate concisely who you are and what you have to offer.
- **What level of experience do you have?**
- Get straight to the facts in the introduction, while avoiding clichés and vague information. This makes for a clear and strong opening statement.
- Aim to tailor your 'Professional Profile' to the prospective role and keep it succinct.

Example:

Dynamic, versatile and results-driven award-winning Career Coach and Entrepreneur. 30+ years' experience gained in HR, Business Development and Career Coaching. Amassed over 1,000 private clients, partnered with global organisations valued at AUS$450M+ Bestselling Author aiming to provide confidence, clarity and effective job searching strategies to help 1,000,000 job seekers to secure sustainable employment.

- **How you help?**
- **Provide evidence of your key achievements**
- The above will set you apart from the competition. It is important you keep this section relevant by identifying the desired **skills and attributes outlined in the job description**, and by ensuring the skills highlighted in your Professional Profile mirror them.
- **Explain your ambitions for the future.**
- Finish by outlining what you are looking to achieve next in your career move. The Hiring Manager needs to know your ambitions are relevant to the opportunity and you're driven and likely to succeed.
- Consider including some personal development goals you are setting yourself in the future. Courses you may be undertaking. Professional development you are considering.

Tip 12

PROFESSIONAL PROFILE: BONUS TIP

- The person conducting your interview may not be the same person who short-listed you for the role.
- They may not have been given or read your original cover letter.
- The Professional Profile briefly outlines your key areas of expertise for them, so they, too, understand who you are and why you may be the best applicant for the job.

Tip 13

INCLUDE THE EMPLOYER CORE VALUES

After looking at relevant job adverts, speak to anybody who may have some insider knowledge about the company and culture. Consider the core values or mission statement on the employer website. Check out the 'About Us' page. If you can't find either on their website, call the employer to find out what they might be.

Employers love to talk about themselves, the up-and-coming projects they are involved in and why they're so marvellous. There are clues for you to follow. Once you understand what the company's core values are, and what the core requirements are for your target roles, you can build these into your resume.

Don't forget, as mentioned earlier: Mirror, mirror, mirror. Include terminology, language and phrases based around the employer's core values to ensure your document generates interest.

Tip 14

QUALITY TRUMPS QUANTITY

- Regarding the presentation of your resume, double-check your document for errors and keep your resume to two to three pages, tops!
- Have you heard of the expression – 'Time Poor?'
- Hiring Managers are normally busy people and are often overwhelmed with job applications.
- Recruiters and Hiring Managers have to make quick decisions based on the details in front of them.
- Nobody has time to read seven pages of a resume. You might find it interesting, but unfortunately, the Hiring Manager doesn't.
- A long resume is in fact a waste of your time. No one will read it.
- Use fewer words to describe achievements. It's another way to help you stand out from the crowd.

Tip 15

SHORT, SWEET, AND TO THE POINT

I love to talk. My husband says my specialised subject is not being a Career Coach, it's 'having a chat.' Cheeky, but probably fair. Yes, I agree, it does sometimes take me a lot longer to get to the point. However, I like to describe all the colourful elements of the story. It's the same with your resume. It's not a platform for the purpose of telling an employer your life story. It is a space to sell yourself. Fast!

- Think short, sweet and to the point!
- The point here being a resume is not one of those places to draw out the information any longer than necessary.
- A Hiring Manager doesn't have the time available to spend reading pages of what you have written.
- Clear, concise and legible resumes are preferred to a resume that looks too jazzy because they can be off-putting when you have to read literally hundreds.
- Choose a clean, simple template (Microsoft Word has heaps of good ones).

- Huge blocks of dark colours take up far too much precious space.
- Two pages ideally, three pages max.
- Ten Years Career History (max).
- The longer the resume, the less likely a Hiring Manager will read it.
- Do not overload it with information.
- Highlight your experience and skills, above all, be succinct.
- Give the best first impression of yourself in your resume.
- Your style of communication should be reflected in your resume.
- It must look neat and address the needs of the advertised role.
- Choose a modern font and style – Size 11 or 12. 10 can be too small.
- Most common types of typeface are Arial and Calibri.
- Each of these is clear and easy to read from a Recruiter's or Hiring Manager's perspective.
- Use bold text to make headings stand out and separate sections with bullet points.
- It is tempting to look creative. Stick to the mainstream.

When conducting research in readiness to share this information with you, I talked to many employers to establish what were the main reasons a job application would be declined. Most explained the first reason was because of errors in either the resume or cover letter.

The second biggest issue was too much irrelevant information, and the resume was far too long.

Take heed!

Tip 16

NO PHOTOGRAPHS PLEASE

Do not include a photograph on your resume unless requested to do so. There are a few exceptions including PR, Modelling, Acting or similar occupations where your facial features may form part of the assessment process.

A personal photo on a resume can give the wrong first impression for many reasons. Unless it has been taken by a profession photographer, you are being employed specifically for the way you look. It is better not to include a photo.

What you perceive to be a great photo could be different to an employer's point of view. Save the photo for your LinkedIn profile. If an employer wants to see a photo of you, they can go to your LinkedIn page and check out your profile photo there.

- Include your LinkedIn URL to show an employer what you look like.

I have seen some unsightly photos on resumes, from a selfie in a car to someone holding the cat.

Top tip: Don't do it!

Tip 17

INCLUDE KEY ACHIEVEMENTS

Below is a list of key achievements to help you build your own examples.

Describe the impact your actions had on the company. Think about what the positive outcome to the business was at the time when you implemented it?

- Draw an employer's attention to your key accomplishments.
- List one additional bullet point at the end of the key responsibilities section titled: **'Key achievement'** for every position you held.
- E.g. Aim to show how you solved a problem, reduced an issue, saved money, increased turnover, implemented an action, created something, increased sales revenue by 10%, 20% or 30%, (include data or numbers).
- Imagine you work in fast food. For every customer you sold a coffee to, you offered a muffin priced at $1 (known as upselling). If you served one hundred customers and fifty of them bought a muffin, you increased sales revenue by 50%.

- Use the 50% to demonstrate how you increased sales revenue.
- By including data, statistics, numbers, facts and figures it looks more impressive and you've elevated your status.
- Remember, you are trying to 'Big Yourself Up.' Almost brag about how great you are here.

If you prefer, you can create a separate space at the top of your resume to bullet point two to three Career Highlights or Career Achievements under the Professional Profile area.

Remember, think about when you have 'added value' to an employer, achieved something at school, received an accolade at TAFE, uni, sporting examples, or something achieved in a personal project.

- Revenue or sales you increased.
- Money you saved the company.
- Time you saved the company.
- Problems you identified and solved.
- Ideas or innovations you introduced.
- Procedures or systems you developed, implemented, or optimised.
- Special projects worked on.
- Industry awards won (i.e., Best Digital Marketing Campaign Award).
- Work-related awards won (i.e., Salesperson of The Year).
- Get strong examples and data.
- Promotions to higher positions you achieved in your job.
- Additional training you completed and professional certifications you received.
- Funding, grants or scholarships you received.

- Popular publications, reports or presentations you (co) authored.
- Blogging and influencing on social media.
- Media coverage you gained for the company.
- Other accomplishments such as volunteering or achievements in sports.
- Work experience and additional skills gained.
- Commendations from clients, managers, senior managers.
- Recognition from groups, peers for tasks you completed well.
- Competitions won.
- Highest achiever year on year.

Tip 18

BE THE SOLUTION TO THE PROBLEM

- Employers are looking for a solution to a problem. You are potentially the solution.
- Describing how you are the solution effectively in your resume will catch the employer's attention.
- It helps to easily identify how you are adding value by creating a solution. That's how you get hired.
- Re-read the job advertisement to identify the purpose of the role.
- Figure out why the position exists. What problem are they trying to fix?
- Once you understand this, you can build your case in the form of your resume.
- Address an employer's expectations by meeting their needs. Explain how you're a great match.
- Demonstrate through your previous achievements, key responsibilities and key accomplishments how you are solution-focused.

Tip 19

BUILD YOUR ANSWERS WITH ACRONYMS

- Acronyms are used regularly by HR teams, Recruiters and Hiring Managers to ask interview questions.
- The aim is to identify how you would behave given a particular set of circumstances.
- An employer is trying to figure out 'If you were in my business and you were faced with this scenario, what would you do?'
- How would you behave?
- Do you have what it takes to complete the necessary task and achieve a successful result for us?
- Used in interviews, they are called Behavioural Style Questions. Determining how you would behave.
- The below acronyms help you build a picture on your resume and when answering questions at an interview.

Here's a simple guide to help you build a picture for an employer.

- **P.A.R.**

Problem – The problem you faced.
Action – What you did to help/resolve the problem.
Result – The positive result you created.

- **C. A. R.**

Challenge – Challenge you faced.
Action.
Result.

- **S.T.A.R.**

Situation.
Task.
Action.
Result.

- **S.A.O.**

Situation you faced.
Action.
Outcome.

I have been using this same example for about thirty years. Remember, you are the star of the show. You are the hero/heroine in a Hollywood movie. Whatever happens, you save the day. No matter how crap the situation, you were the one who created a solution, turned the situation around, and solved the problem. Remember, every example has to start with some kind of challenge or problem and have a successful ending. Like the movies, think 'Happy Ending.'

Tip 20

MAX OUT THE POWER VERBS

When building your resume, remember to sell yourself. Reword your resume to sound more unique and interesting. Point to the action you completed. Begin each of your key responsibilities with an action verb:

Achieved	Decreased	Initiated	Reduced
Acquired	Defined	Inspected	Refocused
Acted	Delegated	Installed	Renegotiated
Adjusted	Delivered	Instituted	Renovated
Administered	Demonstrated	Integrated	Reorganised
Advised	Designed	Intensified	Repaired
Analysed	Developed	Interpreted	Researched
Applied	Diagnosed	Introduced	Restructured
Approved	Directed	Invented	Reversed
Arranged	Distributed	Investigated	Reviewed
Assigned	Doubled	Launched	Selected
Attained	Drafted	Led	Serviced

Budgeted
Built
Calculated
Catalogued
Centralised
Chaired
Classified
Coached
Communicated
Compiled
Completed
Composed
Computed
Conceived
Conducted
Consolidated
Constructed
Consulted
Contracted
Contributed
Controlled
Coordinated
Corrected
Counselled
Created
Edited
Encouraged
Enhanced
Enlarged
Engaged
Ensured
Established
Estimated
Evaluated
Examined
Exceeded
Expanded
Expedited
Formulated
Fostered
Generated
Grouped
Guided
Headed
Helped
Hired
Identified
Implemented
Improved
Increased
Marketed
Mediated
Merged
Mobilised
Moderated
Modernised
Monitored
Motivated
Negotiated
Obtained
Participated
Performed
Persuaded
Planned
Prepared
Presented
Proposed
Provided
Purchased
Recommended
Reconciled
Recruited
Rectified
Reduced
Refocused
Simplified
Sold
Solved
Spearheaded
Specified
Standardised
Started Up
Stimulated
Strengthened
Structured
Trained
Transferred
Transformed
Translated
Turned
Upgraded
Used
Verified
Worked
Wrote

Examples of action verbs demonstrating your skills and abilities:

- **Creativity**: Built, crafted, devised, implemented, pioneered, initiated, established.
- **Efficiency**: Enhanced, advanced, capitalised, maximised, leveraged, improved.
- **Leadership skills**: Headed, coordinated, executed, managed, operated, organised.
- **Improvements:** Refined, remodelled, strengthened, upgraded, transformed.
- **Management skills**: Led, guided, fostered, motivated, recruited, enabled, coached.
- **Bottom line contributions**: Reduced, decreased, consolidated, saved, yielded, increased.
- **Overall achievements**: Awarded, exceeded, outperformed, surpassed, earned, granted.

Remember, these verbs are your prompt to provide an explicit example of a success you've had. It's this proof that will help your resume stand out and show you have the potential to succeed in a new role.

Tip 21

BUILD AN APPEALING CAREER HISTORY

- A resume should include a maximum of ten years employment history. No need to go back further.
- There are some exceptions, but usually you can explain these in one or two sentences.
- On rare occasions I have made a short section called Early Career History and added two or three lines maximum, highlighting the job title and the dates of employment.
- This would be enough information to for an employer to build a picture.
- Start with your job title.
- Next, list the dates you worked for each organisation.
- If you're still employed, put your starting date, then a hyphen, then the word 'present' after hyphen Example: ABC United – present.
- The name of your employer and location.
- It's not necessary to include the full postal address.
- Move onto 'Key Responsibilities' section.

Tip 22

DON'T TELL PORKY PIES

- Be truthful!
- Do not embellish the dates of your previous employment, especially if one of your referees is from the same organisation.
- What will be the consequences if you get caught out telling fibs?
- Be honest, then you can't be caught out.

One of the first questions a referee will be asked is to verify the dates of your previous employment. It does not look good if the dates you have written on your resume are not accurate and don't match up to what your referee confirms.

Tip 23

KEEP IT REAL

- Once again, <u>do not embellish</u> your job titles.
- Inaccuracies regarding your previous level of responsibility, experience or knowledge is not a great way to start a new job.
- You'll feel more confident about the tasks you'll undertake in your new job based on the facts you have provided if you have told the truth.
- Avoid feeling unsettled or nervous in a new job by being factual about what you can and can't do.
- Only state the qualifications you have actually (and legally) obtained.
- Make sure you are working legally with the correct visa or permit regulations.

Employers will expect that what you have stated is fact. If you have stated you are a French interpreter, make sure you can speak French, and can demonstrate your level of skill in this area.

Remember, you could face a test of some kind at interview. Or worse, on the first day of work when you are required to perform duties 'autonomously.' It may be translating documents as part of the induction process.

It would be a tough job if you can't speak French, so keep it real.

When stating a fact on your resume, always ask yourself, *"If I'm tested in this area, can I perform this particular skill as well as I have stated on my resume?"*

If the answer to this question is "No," then don't include it as fact. I have seen employees escorted from workplaces for, let's say, 'errors of judgement' in their resumes.

I have also seen individuals marched off the employers' premises because of inaccuracies relating to legal working rights.

Save yourself time, energy, and potential legal issues. Be factual.

Tip 24

BULLET POINT KEY RESPONSIBILITIES

'Key Responsibilities' is the section title under each position where you provide a brief description of the duties you performed.

List six to seven bullet points (max.) of your most impactful duties. (What did you do?).

- Make this part sound interesting for a Hiring Manager to read.
- Start each bullet point by providing a clear description of what you did using an 'Action Verb' from the list.
- Aim to demonstrate the positive impact your actions had on the business, customer, project or team.
- Keep in mind the needs of the employer and weave in any core values to match their business needs if you can.
- Think about what an employer is asking for?
- Show an employer you have what it takes by describing your relevant experience in this area.
- Be as clear as possible and **avoid jargon**.

- The information on your resume is worthless if an employer has no clue what you are talking about.
- Highlight any specific skills used in your previous role that could be relevant to the job you're applying for.
- Make it clear if this was a voluntary role, secondment, internship or other.

In the key responsibilities area, it's ok to also mention relevant internships and voluntary work too. If you have no paid work history, have you completed work experience, or taken part in a project at school or university? If so, include the project, outcome and skills you needed to use to achieve the successful outcome. Think about how you worked collaboratively with your peers to achieve a desired outcome.

Tip 25

DO NOT COPY AND PASTE YOUR JOB DESCRIPTION

Here's a perfect example of when to ***Get Your Rear into Gear.*** Please make the effort and build your key responsibilities effectively, rather than dumping content from your current or old job description into the career history section.

- Do not copy your last job description and paste it into the career section to describe your responsibilities word for word.
- It looks dull and will not get you on a short-list of candidates.
- In no way does it address the employer needs or match the job you are applying to.
- Go the extra mile and put in the effort. Your efforts will be rewarded.
- It's a lazy way of describing what you did.
- A Hiring Manager or Recruiter will pick up on it straight away and think you have applied zero effort.
- Show an employer how you help, add value, provide a solution, face a challenge, or fix a problem.

Tip 26

INCLUDE ONLY RELEVANT EDUCATION AND QUALIFICATIONS

- Create a separate area in your resume to list your qualifications and/or education.
- State your education and qualifications, certifications or professional training.
- Focus on more recent qualifications.
- Highlight ones that especially relate to the job you are applying for.
- Make sure you state the precise, formal title of the qualifications you have gained.
- It's not necessary to include your grades or marks unless the employer has asked for those details.
- There are some exceptions, but generally, it is fine to leave the details out.
- If you have gained qualifications from a university, always include the name of the university.

Remember, your employer wants to know if you are qualified for the job, so don't include irrelevant courses and qualifications that will clutter up your resume. Especially if they were from way back when.

Tip 27

PEOPLE BUY PEOPLE HELP EMPLOYERS 'BUY INTO YOUR SKILLS'

There is a very famous quote used in sales and marketing saying, 'People Buy People.'

It means if you are a good salesperson, you will be putting the customer's needs first, and appearing more genuine when dealing with a customer. Therefore, the customer is more likely to buy what you are selling because they are buying into your personality first. Hence the 'buying you part.' Effectively, the customer believes the salesperson is selling something to them they need. Rather than the salesperson just trying to sell the most expensive item in the store to make more commission.

Good salespeople are persuasive, listen, and offer solutions to meet a customer's needs, but the secret is that the customer never feels like they are being sold to. So, no hard selling.

Think about the last time you purchased a big item. Was the salesperson nice to you? Did they listen to your needs?

As customers, we enjoy doing business with people we like and trust.

It's the same with employers. They want to work with a genuine, authentic, nice person. (Which I have no doubt you are).

An employer wants to feel good about their hiring decision. They want to trust the person they're about to employ to carry out the duties professionally and responsibly. They don't want to worry about whether the employee is going to be late, or not show up at all.

An employer wants to feel assured the person they're hiring has a strong work ethic, great attitude, and the right skills to carry out the necessary tasks to get the job done.

Effectively, they want to 'buy into' the prospective employee. The same as we might buy into the salesperson.

You are now the sales and marketing person for your own campaign. Ultimately, you will drive your own job searching strategy forward selling your skills for an employer to buy into them. But first, you must familiarise yourself with your skills, what your strengths are, and then learn how to communicate them effectively. In effect, presenting a more persuasive case to the employer. A little like the salesperson. Eventually, persuading the hiring manager to select you.

The first three ways to communicate your skills to an employer are via your:

- Resume.
- Cover Letter.
- LinkedIn profile.

By first identifying your key skills, and establishing what skills the employer is looking for, you can easily highlight those details in your resume, ultimately appearing to be a great match.

You can also 'weave' those skills into the cover letter and include them on your LinkedIn profile.

Tip 28

EMPLOYABILITY SKILLS – WHAT ARE THEY?

Employers look for prospective employees who possess a combination of personal, employability and technical skills. This helps the employer to determine whether the prospective employee has the ability to get the job done and if they can participate effectively in the workplace.

Did you know in 2002, Australian industry took a lead role in describing the skills required to gain and progress in employment?

These were identified in the *Employability Skills for the Future* report, prepared by the Australian Chamber of Commerce and Industry (ACCI) and the Business Council of Australia (BCA) with funding from the Commonwealth Government.

Why do you need to understand what Employability skills are?

These skills are important to help you progress into employment. Showing an employer you have the kind of skills they need to excel in the workplace will highlight your suitability for the role.

A skill is the learned ability to carry out a task. In other words, the abilities we possess. The three categories of skills prospective employers look for are:

- **Personal skills** that relate to our qualities and the ability to work with others.
- **Transferable skills** that can be easily applied across different jobs.
- **Technical skills**, which are those skills required for a specific job.
- **Personal skills** that can contribute to overall employability:
    - Loyalty.
    - Commitment.
    - Honesty and integrity.
    - Reliability.
    - Enthusiasm.
    - Personal presentation.
    - Common sense.
    - Positive self-esteem.
    - A sense of humour.
    - Motivation.
    - Adaptability.
    - Ability to deal with pressure.
    - A balanced attitude to work and home life.

Eight Core Employability skills – These are also called 'Transferrable skills'.

Think about including relevant ones on your resume.

- **Communication**: Contributes to productive and harmonious relations with employees and customers.
- **Teamwork**: Contributes to productive working relationships and outcomes.
- **Problem solving**: Contributes to productive outcomes.

- **Initiative and enterprise**: Contribute to innovative outcomes.
- **Planning and organising**: Contributes to long and short-term strategic planning.
- **Self-management:** Contributes to employee satisfaction and growth.
- **Learning:** Contributes to ongoing improvement and expansion in employee and company operations/outcomes.
- **Technology:** Contributes to effective execution of tasks.

Technical skills: The specialised skills and knowledge required to work in specific occupations and to perform specific duties. The importance and mix of skills will vary from job to job.
Examples of technical skills are:

- Computer Skills.
- Analytical Skills.
- Marketing Skills.
- Presentation Skills.
- Management Skills.
- Project Management Skills.
- Writing Skills.

Remember, the most important reason for listing these skills is to focus on the ones most relevant to the employer's needs. Some employers focus on just two or three workplace skills. Most employers will want you to focus on how you meet their business needs, rather than on your general strengths.

Source: Employability Skills for the Future, 2002
https://australianjobs.employment.gov.au/jobs-future/skills-future

Tip 29

HIGHLIGHT KEY SKILLS

- Create a separate heading and section to highlight your key skills.
- Make them stand out at a glance.
- Present each one in bullet point form.
- Highlight any relevant strengths or professional membership, groups or clubs you are part of demonstrating your alignment to the position.
- IT skills and software packages can be listed separately as they are technical skills.

You can be moved up a short-list of candidates more quickly if you are familiar with an IT package the company has requested as essential or desirable.

Find out which IT packages a company uses. It will save them time if they don't have to train you.

Employers like employees to get to grips with a job quickly and 'hit the ground running.' This could differentiate you from your competitors, especially if you have something they don't have.

The list below can help you build an idea of your skills.

Consider your strengths and experiences that could add value to an employer.

- Begin to 'weave' the strengths and skills into your resume, cover letters and job applications.
- Show an employer your suitability by including some of the skills when describing how you have faced a challenge or created a solution.
- Learn to communicate your skills for the next job interview.

	PERSONAL SKILLS LIST
Able	Talented, bright, having skill to do the job
Accurate	Careful, precise, free from error
Accomplished	Talented, achiever, consummate
Adaptable	Able to adjust well to new situations, having a flexible approach
Ambitious	Aspires to greater things, a strong desire to achieve
Amiable	Likeable, easy to get along with
Analytical	Logical reasoning, critical thinking, deconstruct information into smaller categories
Articulate	Able to express yourself clearly, eloquent
Assertive	Forthright, straightforward, ability to express yourself effectively
Attentive	Pay careful attention
Accurate	Precise, free from error
Bold	Audacious, courageous
Calm	Serene, cool, peaceful

Capable	Accomplished, have the ability to…
Careful	Cautious, hesitant
Collaborative	United approach, team-oriented
Competent	Adequately qualified, possessing the ability, knowledge or skill to…
Confident	Self-assured
Conscientious	Diligent, hardworking, showing care
Consistent	Acting in the same way
Cooperative	Supportive, mutually works towards a common goal
Dedicated	Focused on a goal, devoted
Dependable	Reliable, loyal, trustworthy
Determined	Resolute, purposeful, dogged
Diligent	Meticulous, thorough
Dynamic	Driven, lively, progressive
Efficient	Competent, capable of getting results
Energetic	Active, enthusiastic, spirited
Entrepreneurial	Business-minded, pioneering, ingenious
Flexible	Accommodating, compliant, willing
Hardworking	Strong work ethic, industrious
Independent	Ability to work autonomously, with minimal supervision
Industrious	Hardworking, diligent
Innovative	Pioneering, ground-breaking, new, advanced, original
Knowledgeable	Well-informed, educated, experienced
Motivated	Self-starter, proactive

Optimistic	Enthusiastic, positive, upbeat
Patient	Easygoing, tolerant
Productive	Get lots done, capability to do a lot of work
Realistic	Rational, pragmatic
Reliable	Dependable, steadfast, loyal
Resourceful	Ingenious, solution-focused, problem solver, quick thinker
Responsible	Accountable, trustworthy
Trustworthy	Honest, dependable
Versatile	Multi-talented, resourceful

Tip 30

REFERENCES AND REFEREES

- A referee is the person who will provide your prospective employer with a reference on your behalf.
- They testify to your good character and capabilities, reliability, punctuality, and attendance.
- Most often, your referee will be a direct supervisor or manager.
- You do not have to list your current employer, especially if you don't want them to be contacted.
- The standard expectation is two sets of referee information.
- A key answer a HR person needs to find out is: **Would your previous employer re-employ you?** If the answer could be 'No,' don't put their details on your resume.
- Provide accurate contact details for each person who will be your referee:
  - First and last name.
  - Job title.
  - Name of company.
  - Telephone number.
  - Email address.

- If preferred, add 'references available upon request' and discuss the details at interview.
- Key tip: Only ever provide contact details for someone who will give you a great reference.

If you receive a poor reference, you are unlikely to be offered the job. Moral of the story, when choosing who should provide a reference on your behalf, choose carefully.

Tip 31

HOBBIES AND INTERESTS, OR SPACE SAVER?

With hobbies and interests, only list them if they are professionally relevant unless you are a young person with limited or no work experience.

It's helpful for an employer to see a young person's hobbies if there is limited work experience available. It may be easier for young people to draw upon school, sport, college or Uni examples rather than work.

- Example: If you are applying for a mechanical traineeship, it could be beneficial to highlight relevant hobbies such as reconditioning vintage cars or attending Speedway, demonstrating enthusiasm in that area.
- It is not essential to add hobbies and interests.
- If you are tight for space, leave this section out to fit in more critical details relevant to the job.

Tip 32

SELECT THE RESUME TO FIT YOUR NEEDS

Chronological resume

- A chronological resume is one of the most common resume formats and there's a good reason for it. Employers prefer it because it's straightforward and easy to read.
- Chronological resumes lists your work history in order of date, the most recent position at the top.
- Ideally, it illustrates the progression of a career. The chronological resume format will not work well if you are new to the workforce or if you are changing careers.
- Many employers will decline your resume if they see you do not have enough relevant work experience.
- Try to avoid using a chronological resume if you have lots of gaps in your work history. It will only draw attention to these issues.
- Consider using an alternative style such as a **functional resume** or a **combination resume**.

Functional resume

- A functional resume focuses on your skills and experience, rather than on your chronological work history.
- It is typically used by job seekers who are changing careers, who have gaps in their employment history, or whose work history is not directly related to the job.
- It emphasises specific skills and capabilities to highlight the job seeker's abilities and suitability to the role.
- The focus is shifted from job titles and the amount of time that has passed to the actual skills the applicant possesses. Organise by theme.
- When writing a functional resume, organise your resume by themes, rather than listing your jobs in reverse date order.
- E.g. "Recruiting Experience," and "Customer Service Experience," are grouped with headlines.
- By grouping your skills together, the employer can more easily see that you have the right skills for the job, even if your work history is not related to the job.

Combination resume

- A **combination resume** lists both your skills and your work history first.
- It's ideal for people who want to emphasise their skills over their work history, perhaps because they've changed career fields.
- Employment history is listed next, in reverse chronological order.

- When using a combination resume, you can showcase the skills you have up front that are **relevant to the job you are applying for** while also providing the work history that employers expect to review.

Many employers now find candidates' resumes through search engines, which makes it more important for candidates to use appropriate keywords when writing a resume.

Tip 33

HOW TO BEAT THE ATS

Most large employers use an Applicant Tracking Systems (ATS) to streamline the hiring process. It helps them search, filter, and manage high volumes of resumes. Think about Google Search. It is a search engine looking for keywords you enter. An ATS is much the same.

It is important to understand your resume may now be read by technology first rather than a human being. Good news, you can beat the ATS and here's how.

The ATS is most interested in keywords. The main function of an ATS is to read your resume and compare its content to the relevant job description, looking for the best match. That's why you now have to ensure you tailor your resume for each position you apply for.

- Your resume has to be 'keyword optimised'.
- The ATS is an algorithm and picks out those keywords.
- Your language should mirror the employer's language.
- Choose keywords from the advert to improve your chances of selection.

Tip 34

CREATE A PROFESSIONAL VOICE MESSAGE

Please listen up! This is an important tip, especially if you do not already have a voicemail. I highly recommend getting one ASAP. I am still shocked at the number of job seekers I meet who do not have an answering phone on their mobile phone.

Here's an example of why I believe it is vital for you to have a professional voicemail.

- Imagine this: You have applied for a job, and you are successful and have progressed to the next phase of the recruitment process. The Hiring Manager wants to talk before meeting you face to face.
- He calls you. You are in the shower. You miss the call. He has called from a private number, and he can't leave a voice message. What do you think are the chances of him calling you again? 50/50? Less, I would guess.
- When a Hiring Manager has up to 300 applicants for a role, and has short-listed 30, that's still a lot of phone calls for a person to make.

- The Hiring Manager won't spend much time trying to get hold of you if they are busy.
- Worst of all, bigger companies dial out from private telephone numbers. So even when you realise you have a missed call, you cannot see the number enabling you to find out who called.
- It really is the small things that make a HUGE difference in the job searching process.
- Please record a simple voice message. Create a polite, professional sounding greeting like the example below:
- Hi, thanks for calling Aly Bannister. I'm sorry I'm unable to take your call. Please leave your name and a contact telephone number. I will endeavour to get back to you as soon as possible. Have a great day!
- This is adequate, allowing the Hiring Manager to form a positive first opinion of you. They'll hear your fantastic communication skills, determine a professional impression of you, but overall it allows them to leave a message so you can call them back.

Do yourself a favour. Record a professional voicemail and never miss a future opportunity.

Tip 35

RESUME CHECKLIST

- A document that summarises your work experience, education, skills and achievements.
- It has to be easy to read. Short, sweet, and to the point.
- A winning resume is achievement-focused.
- Include First and Last name(s).
- Contact number – Correct? Get a voicemail!
- Provide a professional email address.
- No need to include your date of birth.
- Don't include your full postal address. Use the suburb.
- Link to your profile – LinkedIn.
- Link to your website – www.
- Use **large, clear, bold** font for your name.
- You don't have to include marital status.
- Add a Professional Profile or Career Summary. A profile is where you stand out from the crowd.
- Who you are? What experience do you have? Why you are qualified to do the job? What value do you bring? Ambitions?

- Consider using words from the Job Description or Advert to beat the ATS.
- Highlight your key skills separately.
- Career History for ten years MAX!
- Two pages in length.
- Career History in reverse chronological order.
- Highlight any roles and elaborate on the ones that are relevant to the job you are applying for.
- Specify: Name of the company you worked for, dates, job title.
- Key responsibilities: A compelling description of what you did.
- Key achievements: Think of awards, recommendations, projects, value of merchandise.
- Use P. A.R. or C. A. R. or S. A. O. method as a guide.
- Education Qualification. Include if relevant.
- Choose people who will provide a great reference on your behalf.
- You don't have to list every job, it's a summary.
- Mature candidates need not share age.
- Treat as a live document, tailor it for every job.

At the end of the book, there is a list of helpful websites where you can find free resume templates to help build a professional document ready for the job searching journey.

Tip 36

CREATIVE COVER LETTERS

A cover letter serves as an introduction, encouraging the employer to read your resume. It aims to show an employer why you are the **right** person for their business. I have written hundreds of cover letters and honestly, the simple, most straightforward ones always get a higher response rate.

- Outlines your suitability for the job.
- Include qualifications, experience, and positive work traits relevant to the job.
- Provides an opportunity to demonstrate your strong written communication skills.
- Tailor your letter to the individual job advertisement. Mirror their language.
- Your first paragraph should hook the reader.
- Try to break up text. Bullet points, font, bold headings. Underline the ref.
- Always include the reference ID or Job number.
- Keep it to a single page. Don't bore the reader.
- Close by thanking the reader.

- Put in a 'Call to Action' requesting an interview (albeit politely).
- Choose a template that matches your resume. Be consistent.
- Proofread, Proofread and Proofread again.
- Two to three paragraphs, or six bullet points maximum unless otherwise requested (Government roles differ).
- Always address the letter personally. Find out the recipient's name (wherever possible).
- Include your contact details twice.

Use a Cover Letter for reverse marketing your details to an employer when they have not advertised a role. It's good to know what you have to offer the employer before approaching them.

I encourage job seekers to create an email cover 'note' for approaching Recruitment Agencies because they are employers too, you know. Agencies handle high volumes of vacancies, so it's great to get them on-board with a short and sweet cover letter showing them why you would be a great representative for their business.

Remember to address the essential criteria in the advert if possible. Be sure to include points addressing the employer's needs.

Check out the employer's website. Try to include words that reflect their core values.

Think Mirror, Mirror, Mirror.

See next example for when you have already spoken with an agency.

Agency Cover Note

EXAMPLE 1

Hi Susie,

<u>Senior Lab Technician or R and D roles – Perth CBD</u>

Thanks for your time earlier today.

Please find attached my Scientific resume highlighting my fifteen years as an experienced Chemist.

Ideally, I'm seeking a part-time position in a Laboratory either as a Research and Development Chemist or Senior Technician, starting early December. I would be most grateful if you could keep me informed of any part-time vacancies coming up. Contract or casual roles along with permanent roles are also a consideration. I aim to be flexible to meet your needs.

Previously I have worked with ABCC Scientific on a contract basis, and ABCC Recruitment casually for twelve months. I'm a 'return to work mum' with impeccable references and a solid work history.

Here's a brief overview of my skills and experience.

- *Five years Research and Development experience.*
- *Eighteen months as a Team Leader and Mentor to junior team members.*
- *Strong Project Management skills.*
- *Graduate Diploma (Research).*
- *Key accomplishment – Promoted to Team Leader status after just six months.*

Thanks for your consideration. I appreciate any feedback you could provide me with.

Kindly contact me on ***0400 000 000.***

Alternatively, if you would like to meet me in person, I'd be happy to call in this week at a time that suits your schedule?

I look forward to hearing from you.

Kind regards,
Aly Bannister
0400 000 000

Once you have defined a list of your key skills and strengths, know your value and what you want to achieve. Then it's time to build your cover letter:

EXAMPLE 2

Cover Letter in response to an Advert
Date
Name
Address
Email and Telephone number
Ms. Smith
Company Name
Address
Suburb State Postal Code

Dear Ms. Smith,

Re: Office Manager – Location and/or Reference Number

Further to your recent advertisement for the above role, please find attached my resume for your review.

Kindly consider my 10+ years' experience as an Entrepreneur and Office Manager, which has required a diverse range of skills including Team Leadership, Advanced Microsoft Office, Bookkeeping, Website design and effective Time Management along with key stakeholder management.

Whilst in regional South Africa, a challenging landscape, my solution-based approach, and flexible attitude proved to be vital. My strong business acumen also proved to be advantageous, when reducing stationery supply costs by 15% at ABC Ltd.

Below are some brief points outlining areas of expertise, hopefully demonstrating how I aim to make a valued contribution to your business.

- *Highly organised with the proven ability to provide senior level administration, operational and technical support to a range of technical departments.*
- *Fully conversant with MS Office Suite, MYOB, ABC Accounts, Quick Books and Adobe InDesign Suite.*
- *Excellent communicator proficient when engaging with clients, management, and liaising with key stakeholders.*
- *Competent at producing effective correspondence, daily, weekly and monthly written reports ensuring a high level of attention to detail.*
- *Extensive experience managing multiple projects at once regularly prioritising time effectively.*
- *Strong comprehension of dealing with urgent project deadlines possessing the ability to provide high quality results in a timely manner.*
- *Exemplary references testifying to my collaborative approach, strong work ethic and team-building skills.*

Thanks for your consideration. I would be delighted to meet you to discuss this opportunity further. Kindly contact me on ***0400 000 000*** *to arrange a time that suit your needs.*

Yours sincerely,
Alison Bannister
0400 000 000

Tip 37

THE HIDDEN JOB MARKET

What is the hidden job market? And why is it so important for a job seeker to learn more about it?

Research tells us that **80-85% of job opportunities are not currently advertised,** which is massive.

The hidden job market is a term used to describe alternative ways of finding a position that hasn't already been advertised. In fact, the vacancy may never get advertised. Therefore, the job is effectively hidden from public view. Hence the hidden part of the phrase.

During a career workshop, participants will often hear me say, *"Australia is a land of great resources. But we still have to dig for the gold."*

It's the same with job hunting. If we really want to unearth the hidden gems in what might appear to be a difficult landscape, we must be prepared to roll up our sleeves and get stuck in.

Successful job seekers have been penetrating the hidden job market for years. I, too, share this information every day with clients who are searching for employment.

- There are a huge numbers of job openings available for those willing to find out where the opportunities exist.
- Learning how to tap into the hidden job market could shape your entire career.
- Many businesses today have hidden jobs. There are lots of reasons they don't advertise.
- An employer may not have time to read hundreds of resumes. Or time to advertise a vacancy.
- Some employers still prefer referrals also known as 'word of mouth' to recruit.
- Many employers use Recruitment Agencies.
- Casual opportunities regularly turn to permanent jobs.
- Voluntary roles often turn into paid employment.
- Work experience can turn into casual paid employment.

Where to start:

- Think of yourself as an investigator or a researcher.
- Be prepared to undertake some research and go on a fact-finding mission. Start with Google.
- Decide what kind of job you want.
- Revisit your 'Employer Wish List' to understand who you are targeting and why you might want to work there.
- Create a timetable for yourself, setting aside time over the coming days and weeks so you're not interrupted. This is serious stuff. You are job hunting.
- Start calling potential employers to introduce yourself ASAP. The first couple of times it might feel uncomfortable, but after a few, the process will get easier.
- Have your resume, cover letter and skills list in front of you to help prompt you when providing answers to employers' questions.

- Being organised will help you feel more confident.
- Find out who the Recruiter or Hiring Manager is.
- Get out there too. Approach employers in person with a copy of your resume.
- Get their name. Follow up with an email. Be courteous.
- Then follow up again with a call if you have not heard back within five to seven days.
- Always be polite and gracious. Thank the person on the phone for their time.
- Be nice to the receptionist. She might own the business.
- Ask for a business card when at an employer site, to help you learn more about the organisation.
- Dress the part. Look smart.
- Utilise your networks. Networking is your #1 opportunity to find a job. Tell people you're available.
- Talk to your friends and family for possible job leads, then make sure you follow up.
- Sell your skills through your social and business contacts. Use Facebook.
- Referrals are a great way of sourcing employment.
- Set yourself a daily goal of how many employers to contact. Start with five or even ten a day.
- Show your interest by conducting research into the business before making an approach.

Imagine yourself being successful very early on in the process. Surely it will have been a short and worthwhile exercise?

Being tenacious is a skill that you will need to develop for this strategy.

Some people are natural go-getters. Others have to work a little harder to earn the same rewards. Throughout history, not every millionaire or billionaire has had qualifications coming out of their ears. Quite the opposite. Many successful CEO's today have virtually no qualifications. However, what they do have is a whole heap of tenacity, self-motivation and self-discipline, by the bucketload.

Being proactive also gives you an edge. The willingness to think outside the box to obtain things your competitors won't have. An eagerness and unwavering belief you can and will achieve your desired outcome and achieve the results others won't achieve will be your ultimate reward.

Some might call it faith. Have faith in yourself and your own abilities. If you believe you will be successful, then you probably will be.

Here's a list of ways to tap into the hidden job market. Use it as a checklist to ensure you have covered all opportunities.

Cold Calling	Make phone calls and visit face to face to introduce yourself.
Reverse Marketing	Create a Cover Letter for reverse marketing purposes. Email it to introduce yourself and attach a resume.
Referrals	Ask friends, family members, ex-colleagues to forward your resume onto Hiring Managers.
Secondments	Put your hand up for opportunities to progress your career.
Career Expos	Bring a resume, collect business cards, follow up by phone/email.
Recruitment Consultants	Research which agencies recruit for your occupation. Connect.

Family members	Talk to wider family members. Where do they work? Who do they know?
Social Groups	Attend social activities. Tell people you are available. Network.
Facebook Groups	Ask your friends who's hiring? Search 'Job Groups' in your city. Check out any career pages locally.
LinkedIn Connections	Share you're available. Ask for tips/referrals/introductions.
EOI	Check out Expressions of Interest. Apply to be in a talent pool (in readiness for when a vacancy comes up).
LinkedIn Groups. Follow companies.	Who are the Recruiters? Connect. Follow. Join the Group.
Voluntary Work	Join voluntary work groups, then ask to be considered for paid work. Give before you receive method.
Industry events and Seminars	Research the next big industry events. Attend. Get business cards. Follow up with emails. Introduce yourself and resume.
Job Alerts	Create Job alerts directly with employers. Look on company websites and Careers Pages.
Employment Providers	Centrelink appoint Employment Providers to help Job Seekers find employment. See if you can join any job clubs or groups.

School Groups	Who is in your school year? Where do they work? Ask them to refer your resume. Ask if they're hiring. Visit the Hiring Manager.
Community Groups	Which community groups are you part of? How do they hire?
Sporting Groups	If you are in a sporting group or club ask other members who they know are currently hiring?

Over the years, hitting the hidden job market has allowed me to create new opportunities for others, providing clients with long-lasting, sustainable jobs and careers. This is an area where you will set yourself apart from the competition. After all, that's the intention, isn't it? To be the candidate of choice in a crowded market? To secure a great job you will enjoy? Being better informed about the hidden job market will increase your chances of finding employment and help you understand where to source and secure future employment opportunities that others may not consider.

Tip 38

REFERRALS 'IT'S NOT WHAT YOU KNOW, IT'S WHO YOU KNOW'

Have you ever heard of this saying?

"It's not what you know, it's who you know."

Basically, it means if you know someone on the 'inside', there is a higher chance of being considered for an opportunity. It could refer to a business opportunity or a job searching opportunity.

Networking is your number one go to—a chance to find employment by leveraging on your connections. People generally refer good people. Why? Because it reflects well on them. It adds to their credibility.

No one is likely to refer an individual who will not be a good match for the job. Otherwise it could reflect poorly on the employee who referred them in the first place, which might not go down well with the boss.

Are you aware some companies still have paid referral schemes in place today to help bring talent into the business? Yes, many do. It is often much cheaper than working with a specialist Recruitment Agency.

I used to work for a bank where they paid a current employee a 'referral bonus' if that employee referred a friend or family member who was successful at interview and stayed in the business for three months. This resulted in a $1500 bonus for the existing employee. Many mining organisations do it too.

So, that's why it is worth talking to your 'network' and asking them to refer you to their employer. Just imagine, if you ask ten people to refer you, and six of your connections do. Then three leads come back to you with an invitation to an interview. Surely, it's a worthwhile exercise? You're accessing job opportunities that have not even been advertised, effectively tapping into the hidden job market.

Tip 39

THINK LIKE A RECRUITMENT CONSULTANT

During my time in Recruitment, this was the number one method of how we would 'secure a placement.' Securing a placement in Recruitment terms means making a good match by matching a job seeker (the candidate) to an employer resulting in a job offer whether it was temporary or permanent.

Reverse marketing is a term used to describe canvassing an employer with a job seeker's details when a vacancy has not been advertised. The aim is to have the employer consider the particular job seeker's resume for any new or upcoming vacancies. If we class the job seeker as a high-calibre candidate, and the employer has a genuine need for their skill set, often employers create a vacancy or opportunity to address the needs of their business.

Some employers literally do not have the time to advertise a vacancy. Therefore, if a Recruitment Consultant contacts them with a great job seeker's details, the employer will engage with the job seeker there and then.

Now let's pretend for a moment that you are a Recruitment

Consultant. You will be the one who contacts the employer directly, to Reverse Market your own details. Just imagine, your proactive approach could impress the employer.

There is a lot of success to be made in this area. Sometimes it's a matter of being in the right place at the right time! Voila! Meaning as if by magic something appears. For you, that's an all-important job offer.

Multi-national Recruitment Agencies are fully aware of how successful the Reverse Marketing strategy is when applied correctly. It can, and more often than not, does work. Huge businesses across the globe have literally built their empires on it. National and multi-national organisations have grown from small boutique Recruitment Agency style businesses to massive global organisations. Because they have systematically stuck to this plan. The senior managers in charge of these companies fully comprehend the positive effects of how this straightforward system works.

Consider this for a moment. If it works for them, it can work for you.

Reverse marketing can be an effective tool for finding employment. Yes, it takes a bit of courage to get started. Courage, coupled with a sense of optimism and self-belief to create an opportunity for yourself that on the surface, may not have previously existed. But what a worthwhile exercise when you secure an offer of employment. Even a work trial leading to a paid ongoing position. Or an interview with a job offer at the end of it.

Surely it has to be worth giving it a go, doesn't it?

Needless to say, I have loved and still love helping individuals, just like you, to secure employment. This is just one tip I share every day. You can do this. I fully appreciate it will not work every time. But guess what? It can and does work regularly for all those Recruitment Agencies out there. Just count how many of them are in the Yellow Pages. That will demonstrate why there are so many of them in business today.

Almost every day, when coaching clients on a one-to-one basis, I repeat the below phrase.

"You must be willing to do the things today others don't do in order to have the things tomorrow others won't have."

Les Brown, the American motivational speaker.

This is a brilliant quote, especially because it is so relevant when it comes to job searching. It has helped me stay on track when the going gets tough. And I hope it will help you too and remind you of the goal you're aiming for. The purpose of why you started out on your job search quest in the first place.

Whilst Reverse Marketing your own details might feel a little uncomfortable at first, as loads of new processes often do, the rewards for your efforts will pay off big time. That's because you are considering alternative ways of finding employment that many of your competitors have not contemplated or are not willing to consider.

My father, an 'old-school type', born in Northern Ireland in the 1930s, and a man who could appear fairly stern at times, had an insightful phrase. One I also apply today in my workshops.

"Learn how to put your arse out of shape."

Samuel Donaghy, Snr. Philosopher and astute ld-timer.

It's like the Les Brown quote, meaning you should push yourself out of your comfort zone. Get up off your backside and get cracking. There is no time like the present to wrestle with an opportunity. Get moving now! View every day as a new chance to succeed. What can you do today to progress your aspirations one step further in the right direction? Take the blinkers off. Think like a Recruitment Consultant.

Tip 40

CONNECT WITH A RECRUITMENT CONSULTANT

Now you are aware of how Recruitment Agencies work, this is a good time for you to contact Recruitment Agencies in your area to introduce yourself and find out what types of roles they are hiring for.

I will just recap on some of the ways they may help you. Again, tapping into the hidden job market.

- Recruitment Agencies broker a relationship with an employer. That could be at a local level, or at a state-wide level, or on a national level to find the business a candidate (another word for job seeker).
- Employers hire Recruitment Agencies to find job candidates and pay them a finder's fee.
- Recruitment Consultants identify qualified people, screen the candidates, and provide support to the employer during selection of the new hire. They do this by sending resumes, coordinating interviews, checking references, collating foundation documents, making the job offer on behalf of the employer.

- For a permanent vacancy, the Recruitment Agency gets paid by the employer, normally a fee of approx. 15% - 20% of a candidate's first annual salary, but this can go as high as 30% for a hard to fill position.
- If a Recruitment Agency finds a temporary candidate for an employer, the candidate gets paid by the agency. The agency charges the employer a much higher hourly rate. E.g. the candidate gets paid $25 per hour. The Agency charges the Recruitment company $45 per hour.

Hopefully, the above explanation will help you build a picture of why there are so many Recruitment Agencies around, and how they could help you get a job.

If you have the skills they are looking for, they can promote you to one of their employers (customers) and get paid for doing it. Additionally, it encourages brand loyalty from their customer (the employer). If one agency produces great employees, the employer is more likely to use them again and again.

One tool I provide to all of my clients is a database of all the Recruitment Agencies in their area, specialising in their type of work. They then set off (as part of their homework) and contact every single one to find out whether they have a suitable vacancy. Or if not, once they have established a rapport, and decide if a candidate is suitably qualified, the Recruitment Agency will 'Reverse Market' their details to one of their existing employers.

Recruitment Agencies are always looking for good representatives for their business to promote to an employer because that's how they make money. Plus, it's a competitive world and they want to make more money than the other agencies, so they want to find a constant stream of good candidates or local 'Talent' to represent their agency.

If an agency engages with you, and you let them down, it is highly unlikely they will ever use you again, unless there are extraordinary circumstances. An agency can easily lose their client if the candidate doesn't show up for work. It's a ruthless business.

Ideally, you will now see the benefit of speaking to not just one, but several Recruitment Consultants from different agencies in your area to identify the kinds of roles they are currently recruiting for. This establishes whether you would be suitable and if they could help to find you a job faster.

Please don't be fooled. I make it sound easy, but it's not always easy to broker a relationship with a Recruitment Consultant because they have hundreds of candidates on in their database looking for work. But you must at least try.

- Firstly identify all the agencies in your area and learn what roles they specialise in.
- Set aside time to contact each.
- Phone them first so they can hear what a great communicator you are and learn more about you.
- Find out the Recruitment Consultant's name and email address.
- Send them your resume directly if you can.
- You will also probably need to register on their database by creating a login.
- Follow up with a call within a few days.
- Do not use the 'Hit and Run method', meaning you should speak to them more than once, and follow up your application to develop a rapport. Just applying for a job and expecting to hear back from the Recruitment Consultant is not advised. Apply effort, follow up every application and be courteous. You are then more likely to

receive a call back or email from them.

- They are working on your behalf. Contact them weekly. Show you are motivated and can be relied upon.
- Next, keep looking on their websites for vacancies being advertised. There may be one you want to apply for.
- Keep in regular contact. Be polite and as flexible as possible to meet their needs.
- Have all your foundation documents ready. After all, they are potentially your next employer.
- Above all, make it easy for them to engage with you.
- Check out agencies and Recruitment Consultants on LinkedIn. It's another way of connecting.

One of the key benefits of working with a Recruitment Agency is the speed in which you can find work.

If they have a vacancy matching your skill set, you could start a temporary or a temporary to permanent role within days. It happens regularly. So please seriously consider the benefits of undertaking this exercise.

Tip 41

GET ONBOARD WITH LINKEDIN IN TWELVE EASY STEPS

LinkedIn is another great way of finding employment. One your competitors may not have considered. It's about leveraging on your opportunities and getting ahead of the game.

Spreading your job search across different job boards increases your chances of landing a job. You will see different jobs advertised on different sites. LinkedIn has its own jobs board where you can search and apply for jobs directly.

When I first meet clients, many tell me they don't even know how to use LinkedIn. That's O.K. Everything is easy when you know how. Start today.

Be mindful you could miss out on a whole heap of job opportunities every day if you're not onboard.

The good news is, it's pretty straightforward to use. Think Facebook, but with a workplace etiquette (no naughty language or inappropriate behaviour).

There are huge benefits of being on LinkedIn. Here's an overview of how it works:

- 575+ million users worldwide in 200 countries – all building connections for employment.
- It's known as a social networking site for professionals.
- Jobs advertised every day for all sorts of positions, not just high-level roles (it's changed a bit).
- Hiring tool for Recruiters and Hiring Managers to find Talent (job seekers) like you.
- Employers share insights into their business in newsfeed, daily and weekly (making it easier for you to engage).
- People in your network can introduce you to potential employers. Or send you InMail regarding job opportunities. (I send my connections jobs all the time).
- A place to showcase your skills, achievements, qualifications, work experience and a photo.
- Elevates your digital brand.
- Less competition when applying for jobs unlike some other job boards.
- A way to tap into the hidden job market. Build a rapport with future employers who aren't advertising.
- 150+ million groups on LinkedIn. Join groups to get tips on who is currently hiring.
- Keep informed of industry insights, projects coming up, trends and employment latest news.
- Automate your job searching. Large employers use 'LinkedIn Recruiter' as a tool to find job seekers just like you.

Since Covid-19, LinkedIn introduced a new feature worth checking out. Visit **www.linkedin.com**

The first page you see allows you to search for a job, and you don't even have to have a profile. How good is that? You can search for people you know. Learn about new skills too. Online learning is the way of the future.

When you are ready to build a basic profile, here's an example of how to simply use LinkedIn to help you find employment:

1. Create a profile, include e-mail address, employment history, skills, hobbies and voluntary work.
2. Summary section: 2000 characters, boast of accomplishments, key skills, inject personality, max it out to catch an employer's attention.
3. Build an attractive headline to entice employers to want to learn more about you. 120 characters!
4. Add a professional-looking photo. Employers are eleven times more likely to engage with you when they see your face. Look smart!
5. Include a video in your summary and relevant experience sections to stand out from the crowd.
6. Create an **#OpentoWork** feature. Frame your photo so employers can see you're available. Link below.
7. Build connections: friends, ex-colleagues, current or ex-managers, peers from school, uni alumni.
8. Search for hashtags relevant to your area of work or interest. #jobtips #employment #careers
9. Use the free account first. You don't have to use Premium and it works well (I use basic).
10. Follow employers where you would like to work. Join Groups to learn more about industry insights, professional chatter, etc.
11. Research people you want to emulate. See what they have written. Follow their framework.

12. Change privacy setting so employers and recruiters can easily find you.

#OpentoWork feature

Search the link below to watch a 1-minute video on how to utilise the new feature to help employers identify you're available for new opportunities.

https://www.linkedin.com/help/linkedin/answer/67405/let-recruiters-know-you-re-open-to-work?lang=en

LinkedIn Premium has account options for job seekers, sales and talent professionals, and the general professionals who want to get more out of LinkedIn. If you have a free account and want to upgrade, you can compare account types, but there is a charge to be part of LinkedIn Premium ranging from the following.

$29.99 to $59.99 for job seekers. $79.99 for sales professionals. $119.95 for Recruiters.

Consider this, if Recruiters are paying $119.95 per month to be on LinkedIn, it has to offer value for money in terms of the return it provides for them. They are paying to find talent. Remember, you are the talent.

My suggestion would be for you to use basic first. Become familiar with it. Then decide at a time in the future whether you need to have LinkedIn Premium.

I am connected with many Career Coaches and Career Industry leaders, organisations and groups. That's because when they post information I believe could be valuable and potentially be beneficial to a jobseeker in some way, I will share the content.

For example, when I learn about a new tip or piece of information relating to 'Who's Hiring' at present, I share it in my newsfeed. That's so my community can view the details and hopefully progress their job searching opportunities further.

One final fun thing I will mention, connect with people you really like too. Or people who you can learn from. I follow Oprah, Tony Robbins, Bob Proctor, Hal Elrod and the Queen amongst plenty of others. If they're all on it, then surely there must be a pretty good reason to use it. Start connecting today. Connect with me if you like.

Tip 42

FAILING TO PLAN IS PLANNING TO FAIL

What is your plan to succeed in today's job market? If you don't already have one, now is the time to ***Get Your Rear into Gear*** and create a plan.

There is a famous quote by Sir Winston Churchill, former UK Prime Minister during World War II.

"Failing to plan is planning to fail."

Meaning, if you do not have any kind of career or job searching plan, you may find yourself failing quickly. Something I would like you to avoid at all costs.

A career and action plan can help you progress more rapidly and achieve short, medium, and longer-term goals. A simple plan or template to keep you on track is what I'm asking you to prepare.

Consider this example used as part of everyday normal life.

Bank Managers love a business plan.

The first question any half decent Bank Manager will ask you before lending you money or providing you with a business loan is this: **"Do you have a business plan?"**

Bank Managers want to know whether you are genuinely aiming to succeed in business, and if you'll be a safe bet when it comes to getting their money back.

Therefore, if you don't have a plan, it shows the bank you are not serious about succeeding. So, they probably won't lend you any money in the first place. By not having a business plan, it tells the bank you haven't necessarily thought through your business idea thoroughly enough to determine how you're going to either make money, grow the business or market your product. But above all, be able to pay the money back.

As a result, it's unlikely to be considered as fitting the lending criteria of being a solid investment.

Basically, the bank will not consider your business as a safe bet if you can't be relied upon to pay back the loan.

Guess what? It's the same when job seeking. You need to be clear on what your outcome looks like. To succeed, you will need a plan. Otherwise, how do you plan on finding a job?

Everyone's circumstances are very different. It may take you a relatively short amount of time to find employment as opposed to let's say your friend. Because you are unique. Your personality is different to anybody else's, your skills, qualifications, and experience differs too.

Alternatively, it may take a while before you land the job you're really hoping for because it requires more cultivating. You have to plant the seeds first, and it may take a lot longer to see the results because you might need to undertake research, further professional development, and/or some kind of training.

Making connections with the right employers, establishing a rapport, or networking in the right circles can take extra time. You may need to have a longer lead time to build up to securing the ideal position. Or at the very least get invited for an interview.

Recently I worked with a client and we allowed thirteen weeks from the beginning of the job searching strategy to the end. This gave us enough time in the lead up to find the job of her dreams. I told her at the beginning it would probably take that length of time. In fact, it was thirteen weeks to the day that she received the written job offer for the ideal position she'd been searching for. It's great when that kind of thing happens. I call it 'Text Book stuff.' Especially because she was a 'star pupil' and did everything I asked of her to progress in the right direction. She was truly tickled pink. I must admit, I was thrilled too.

Two weeks earlier, I partnered with another client who explained she wanted to secure an Accounts/Admin role locally as a stepping stone job for the next one to two years. She wanted to obtain qualifications in the evenings in readiness to secure her bigger career goal.

I explained to her that if she followed the straightforward instructions provided, and did everything I asked of her, (building her Employer Wishlist, defining her non-negotiables, connecting with Recruitment Agencies) she could be working within the fortnight. On this occasion, she was in total disbelief. I explained, let's have some fun with this and see where this exercise takes us.

Almost begrudgingly, she did exactly what I suggested. She dedicated time to the job searching strategy we devised around the times when her baby was sleeping. Routinely telephoning each Recruitment Agency on the list I provided and introducing herself verbally. She also followed the brief script I'd given her.

I explained to her at the very beginning, *'You have to be in it to win it.'*

Meaning, unless you participate, how will you even know whether you're going to be successful? However, she thought I made it all sound too simple.

She was surprised when within two days of her initial contact with every agency; she received a call back. Then came a short phone screen, which resulted in a job offer for a temporary to permanent contract starting the very next week. Hallelujah! I exclaimed.

The next time I heard from her was in the form of an email after she bought work clothes for her new job starting the following Monday. She, too, was tickled pink.

The point here is this. Please aim to be open-minded to suggestions and consider all the options in your path because you never know what opportunities await you until you try.

It's time we get started. Whatever your circumstances, it's always best to have a plan.

Tip 43

WHAT DO I NEED TO SUCCEED?

Questions to ask yourself from the beginning of the process to help you make sure you have everything covered.

Here's some food for thought. Listed below are some questions to help you think about where to start. It's important to embark as quickly as possible, let's say, to get the 'ball rolling' and then continue to drive the process once you begin. Time is of the essence.

These questions are aimed at stirring up thoughts you may not have previously considered. It's also a great time to brainstorm your answers or drafting your answers in your 'Employment Book' to help you become clearer on what your outcome is going to look like.

Start by establishing:

What do you intend to achieve at the end of your job searching journey? Now or in the future.

Imagine what the outcome looks like. How would it feel when you achieve it? Keep in mind the rewards and benefits at the end of the journey to remain enthusiastic and motivated.

If you are determined to start a job in the next few weeks, what steps are you prepared to take over the coming days and weeks to achieve concrete results?

- What actions are you going to take now to guarantee success in the long-term?
- Have you built your 'Employer Wishlist'?
- Have you developed your list of 'Non-negotiables'?
- Who do you want to work for?
- What job do you want to do?
- Why do you want to do it?
- Are you clear on how much you need to earn?
- What will be expected of you in the role?
- What do you have to offer the employer?
- Have you considered your Employee Value Proposition?
- If you are not experiencing success at present, what needs to change?
- Which areas do you need help with?
- Who can help you?
- What will you do today to progress your career journey and get one step closer to achieving a job offer?
- Have you identified the ideal company you would like to work for?
- Are you looking for a stepping stone job or a long-term opportunity?
- Have you set up job alerts directly with multiple employers so you will be one of the first to hear about a vacancy?
- How do you intend to connect with an ideal employer?
- How many Recruitment Agencies might you contact?
- Which Recruitment Agencies does the company you want to work for use, if any?

- Have you connected with relevant Recruitment Consultants either verbally or on LinkedIn?
- Have you set up the job alerts feature on LinkedIn?
- Have you downloaded more than one job board app such as Seek or LinkedIn on your mobile? Glass door? Career One?
- How many digital profiles are you going to set up on jobs boards?
- Who would you like to emulate?
- Do you need assistance to build your LinkedIn profile?
- Have you set aside some specific time to spend working on your LinkedIn profile?
- Who can help to build or create your resume?
- Are you familiar with addressing Key Selection Criteria? If not, who can help you?
- Who can help write and perfect your 'Elevator Pitch'?
- How many quality job applications are you going to complete today, this week, this month. What's the goal?
- How many calls are you going to make directly to employers?
- Have you diarised next action steps and follow-up calls?
- Which type of job suits your level of physical fitness?
- What kind of work suits your key skills?
- Have you joined any job searching or career groups on Facebook?
- Who in your circle of friends knows you are looking for work?
- Have you made a list of everyone in your network?
- Have you set a target to connect with everyone in your network?

- Have you created a timetable to set time aside for dedicated 'job hunting'?
- Have you spoken to any Recruiters in the HR department advertising a position and asking for a full position description?
- Consider whether you would be suited to the type of work?
- Have you thought about evenings, weekends, shifts or different patterns of work?
- Have you created a simple pitch for Reverse Marketing purposes when contacting employers?
- Have you created your list of strengths and skills?
- Who do you know that could help to advance your job searching efforts?
- Are you in touch with a Jobs or Skills Centre?
- Are there any very short, affordable courses available to help you secure employment more quickly?
- Are there any free workshops available to assist with employability skills?
- Have you spoken to your local libraries?
- Have you checked out Eventbrite for free online webinars or face-to-face workshops to help tailor your resume, provide career guidance, assist with cover letters or build a LinkedIn profile?
- Are there any employment providers, career coaches or career guidance services who you can talk to locally or virtually?
- How about talking to the services at the School, TAFE, University or College?
- Do you need to involve anyone else to initially support you to free up your time and provide you a little space and time to get cracking?

- Enlist the help of a parent to help give you guidance or ideas and provide encouragement.
- Need the help of a friend to proofread your resume, cover letter or job applications?
- Is there somewhere quiet where you will be left undisturbed to conduct research for job searching?
- Can you visit the local library to help eliminate distractions and increase your productivity levels?
- Have you checked out all the government online Job Seeker assistance tools? See Useful Websites to consider in Australia in the back pages.
- Have you checked out many of the free Career Advice pages? Glassdoor Career Advice page, Indeed Career Advice, Seek Career Advice.
- Have you created a plan on paper to identify your short, medium or long-term career goals?
- Have you developed your S.M.A.R.T. goals for the short or long-term?

These questions are aimed at helping you to set yourself up for success. Whatever happens, you must be clear on how you can add value to an employer.

Several of these practices will take time and careful consideration. It's best not to rush things. Quality trumps quantity.

I hope you find the list of questions advantageous, providing you with a starting point. These are habits that once you practice, they can better serve you both in the short and long-term.

Hopefully, you will be moving into the interview phase next. More on that in Tip 48.

All these small things add up to building your **platform for success.**

Tip 44

EMPLOYER CONTACT LIST AND VACANCY TRACKER

Save yourself time during the job searching process by keeping track of all the vacancies you are applying for and any reference numbers relating to the vacancy. It will help to keep you organised and act as a reminder of when to put in a follow-up call to determine how your application is progressing.

There are many benefits to keeping a record of the employers you are actively talking to. It saves the hassle of continually 'Googling' to find the employer website for the contact details.

In case you forget the HR telephone number or the name of the person you have spoken to, it keeps the details in a neat format, quickly accessible for you to find. Maybe you scribbled the telephone number down on a piece of paper and just can't find it now. Well, this will have you covered.

In addition, when you receive a call back from the employer for the crucial job interview, it reminds you of who you have been in contact with. You'll also have any extra information you recorded during the initial discussion in the comments section.

You can simply build your own Employer Contact List and Vacancy Tracker in Word or Excel.

Here's an example of what to include in the headers:

Date, Contact Name, Company, Vacancy Title, Comments and F/U column.

Alternatively, go to **www.alisonbannister.com** to download a free copy.

Make sure you follow up every job application you make with a phone call or email to show you're super motivated and keen to progress. You may not be the only applicant, but you might be the only person who called them to follow up and they may even ask you to come in for an interview. It happens.

Tip 45

CRAFT YOUR CAREER GOALS

Once you have devised a plan, and you're clear on what you are prepared to do and developed a timetable for the coming days and weeks, the critical part is to then stick to the plan.

These days we hear quite a lot about goals and how to achieve them. When you are looking for employment, it's important to have some clear objectives in mind to help you gravitate towards accomplishing an end result. Effectively, give yourself the chance to progress every day towards the goal.

- A goal can be described as the object of a person's ambition, aim or desired result.
- A career is described as an occupation undertaken for a significant period of a person's life.
- A career goal can be described as a job or a long-term employment opportunity that services your needs and provides you with an outcome.
- What does accomplishing a goal mean for you?

Below is a great quote I hope will give you some assistance in sticking to your plan, aiming to inspire you to take action and achieve your goal.

"A *goal is a dream with a date. A dream written down with a date becomes a goal. A goal broken down into steps becomes a plan. A plan backed by action makes your dreams come true." Greg Reid*

When you secure employment, ideally, you will have the opportunity to reach the desired outcome which could be buying a car, boat, house or even going on a holiday. Effectively, any reward that holds meaning for us, the object of our desires.

It's fair to say not everyone understands the purpose of even having a goal. Below is a brief explanation to illustrate why they can work.

Setting **goals** helps you trigger new behaviours, helping you to guide your focus and sustain a certain level of momentum in life. Goals also help align your focus and promote a sense of self-mastery.

I personally set goals daily because it brings more of a sense of urgency around completing a task. Therefore, I get more done and become more productive when I follow my daily goals or my 'To-do List.'

- In business, employers set goals for their workforce every day. You may already have experienced KPI's or Key Performance Indicators. Basically, they are targets. And guess what another word to describe a target is? A goal.
- The purpose of having a goal is to keep us motivated and on a trajectory that enables us to achieve the things we set out to accomplish in life, ultimately feeling more fulfilled and rewarded.

- A goal has to be personal to you and not be someone else's goal either. Otherwise you will feel less compelled to take action because it has no real meaning for you. Whereas if it's your own personal goal, you are much more likely to try to achieve or accomplish it.
- Maybe professional development, a promotion, a traineeship or an apprenticeship is your goal. Or a rewarding job with a great team culture or working with an ethical employer is your dream job.
- A position that leaves you feeling fulfilled and part of the team. Everyone's dream job or goal should be personal to them.

Whatever goal you intend to achieve, it will help to write it down. Then attempt to look at the goal as often as possible. This will remind you during the job searching process of the benefits potentially within your grasp when you eventually accomplish what you have set out to do to reach your goal.

Seeing your goal, then believing you can achieve it is the starting point to achieving any goal. However, now it's time to do the necessary work to achieve your goal. You must take action.

Maybe your initial goal is finding a part-time job to fit around your family, schoolwork, or university studies. Potentially a final job leading into retirement, or a new role that will transition onto another career path entirely. Possibly a stepping stone job whilst thinking about the bigger career goals. Or you may be aiming to land an interview to become a Trainee or Apprentice. Alternatively, you could be aiming to become the next CEO or General Manager of a company you've been angling towards for years.

Whatever your goal looks like, it may be worthwhile to consider using a method like the S.M.A.R.T. goal framework.

When writing a S.M.A.R.T. goal, you work through each of the letters to build a goal to identify exactly what needs to be accomplished, when it needs to be accomplished by, and how you'll know when you're successful. A S.M.A.R.T. goal helps focus your efforts and increases the chances of achieving the outcome.

A goal should be:

- **S** – Specific
- **M** – Measured
- **A** – Achievable
- **R** – Realistic
- **T** – Timed

S.M.A.R.T. goals can help you progress towards your own career goal and personal goals. S.M.A.R.T. goals are used frequently in business too. Nowadays, when employees sit down for their performance review, more often than not, a discussion will take place about what the employee intends to achieve over the coming months. What action is the employee going to implement to complete a project or set of tasks. Regularly, some form of goal template will be used.

To successfully achieve a goal:

- Do one thing every day that will bring you closer to a sense of accomplishment.
- Determine what you want to achieve.
- Break down how you will get there.
- Write it down.
- Stick to your plan.

Tip 46

THE 7 P'S AND INTERVIEW PREPARATION

One workshop I continue to facilitate on a regular basis is called *Interview Success – Tips and Tricks*. This program aims to better prepare candidates for what they might face when an employer invites them to attend an interview.

Preparation for an interview starts well before the actual day itself. In my view, it should start days if not weeks before the interview is due to take place. Why? Here's just one example.

If you truly want to improve your interview performance skills, settle your nerves, reduce the feelings of anxiety or tension and increase your levels of confidence, the key is to: **Prepare, prepare, prepare!**

There is an old British Army adage relating to the 7 P's you may already be familiar with.

'Proper Planning and Preparation Prevents Piss Poor Performance.'

The British Army used to apply this motto when preparing

troops for battle or life and death situations. The good news is that you're not about to face either a battle or a life and death situation. After all, it is an interview. (Albeit one you want to ace).

Now, it is fair to say I dilute the language when talking to clients as per the example below. But the point is, preparation is needed to succeed. If you choose to not adequately prepare, the outcome will speak for itself. Try to understand this.

- The outcome of your interview will depend entirely on the preparation and effort you put in beforehand.
- Your performance will influence the Hiring Manager's decision.
- The outcome of any performance is a testament to the effort applied in preparation.
- A great performance demonstrates to an employer you have taken the time to put the work in.
- A poor performance confirms to an employer you probably haven't.

Poor Preparation results in Poor Performance.

Whichever phrase resonates with you the most, use the one that will help you remember to put the effort in to get the tangible results out.

Take the necessary time to undertake the prep work in advance to stand a greater chance of being selected as the preferred candidate and progressing to the next stage.

If you choose to 'wing it' (I've seen plenty who have, and they failed miserably as a result), the chances are you will not progress to the next stage of the recruitment process. Whether that's a second or third interview, testing phase, trial, or moving to the verbal and subsequent written job offer, do yourself a favour and put in the 'legwork.'

Success comes about from being organised and putting thought into how you want to be perceived by the person interviewing you on the big day.

The following is a guide for how you might make the best possible impression.

Tip 47

PREPARATION BUILDS CONFIDENCE

Prepare

Preparation before an interview is vital if you want to be successful and obtain a job offer. Why?

- Ultimately, to get hired.
- Demonstrate you have the skills, knowledge, and experience to do the job.
- To outshine your competitors.
- Be taken seriously.
- Show you are motivated, and you want to work there.

The more you know about yourself and the skills you possess, the more confident you will feel.

The more you know about the employer, the more knowledgeable you will appear.

Prepare your interview responses in advance (drafted in your Employment Book) to present an accurate and relevant profile, whilst also selling your skills and experience.

Consider all those times when you have faced a challenge or problem or tricky situation at work or whilst in education, or at home. Think about what you did to overcome the issue. Remember what actions you implemented to solve the problem. Then illustrate the positive outcome (or happy ending). Provide a quick example of how you created a great outcome because of your quick thinking or positive actions.

Practice your responses to interview questions. This will enable you to be confident and clear in your answers. Look in the mirror when you are doing it. Stand upright and project your voice.

Communicating effectively shows an employer you have a level of confidence in your own abilities.

Nobody knows what an interviewer is going to ask you on the day. To help formulate your answers, use the acronyms mentioned earlier. Break down the question in your head and build your answers. Remember the following technique.

P.A.R. Problem Action Result
C.A.R. Challenge Action Result
S.A.O. Situation Action Outcome
S.T.A.R. Situation Task Action Result

Whichever acronym you choose, any of them will help you explain the challenge or problem or situation you faced.

Research

Take the time to find out about the company's history, performance, and organisational structure. They will almost certainly ask why you want to work there or what you know about the company.

Find out as much as you can about the company's market, their products, or services.

Start with Google. Follow the company on LinkedIn. View relevant profiles of their employees. Learn more about their size or location. See if you can find company reviews. Check out articles in newspapers or magazines.

All of your research will help you demonstrate your knowledge to impress the interviewer. It will also help when you are asked one of the first questions that normally comes up.

"What do you know about our organisation?"

If you have done some research, you should be able to answer this question comfortably.

Plan

Planning happens before the interview. Plan for enough time to get there, have directions and remember the name of the person you will meet. Google Maps is a useful tool to find your destination.

- Bring the contact details of the interviewer with you. Just in case you need to tell them you're running late.
- Make sure you know the interviewer's name and email address.
- If it's a tricky name, call ahead beforehand to ask someone how to pronounce it correctly. The interviewer will be impressed if you get it right first time.
- Read the interview instructions twice. Are you familiar with where the interview is taking place?
- Leave extra time to reach your destination if you are unfamiliar with the location.
- Have Plan B ready in case your transport lets you down.

- Transport. How will you get there?
- What's the address where the interview will be held?
- What's your Plan B?
- Plan to arrive fifteen minutes early. It's a good start to any interview, showing your enthusiasm.
- Setting the scene for a positive interview. It's important to give a brilliant first impression. Don't be late. Look good, feel great.

Tip 48

PHONE INTERVIEWS

When you get invited for a phone interview, (and I'm imagining that you will) please take into consideration where you intend to conduct it. An interviewer can hear everything.

- Choose a quiet and appropriate setting with no interruptions.
- Have good coverage on your phone.
- Be upbeat and friendly. This helps to sound enthusiastic and motivated.
- Smile when you dial. The interviewer can tell if you are happy to be there. It also helps to build rapport.
- Be organised. Note pad and pen to make notes or give yourself prompts to answer tricky questions.
- Have your resume in front of you, list of strengths and key skills as a quick reminder.
- Put post-it notes on your wall/laptop. Visual prompts to help you remember key points to discuss.
- Stand up to be physically bigger, which can help to make you feel and sound more confident.

- Do not eat/drink/chew gum/smoke or swear.
- Avoid tapping a pen or pencil.
- Keep two things in your mouth – your tongue and teeth.
- Listen carefully to the whole question and do not butt in.
- Remember to ask questions and always finish by thanking the person.
- It is O.K. to ask about the next stage, or when are you likely to hear an outcome.
- Try to enjoy the experience. It will help to handle your nerves.

Tip 49

FACE-TO-FACE INTERVIEWS

First impressions are important when attending a face-to-face interview. Personal presentation is critical.

Ask yourself this. When was the last time you tried on your interview clothes? Do they still fit?

I have had conversations with candidates on the phone whilst they've been in a changing room trying on new clothes twenty minutes before their interview. That's because they hadn't realised their regular interview outfit no longer fitted them. Or they broke the zip on their trousers or dress. Yep, it happens.

We may all have some extra curves going on after lockdown. So, it's best to check the details of your outfit well in advance. Small things like getting your interview clothes in order will make a big difference to how you handle your nerves on the day. You want to eliminate any elements that will detract from your success. Remove anything extra to worry over, giving yourself more time to focus on the more important elements of the interview such as your performance during the meeting.

It's all about taking the pressure off yourself and not adding to it at the last minute.

There's nothing worse than putting yourself under extra pressure. We can all act a little strangely sometimes when feeling under pressure. You do not want to end up appearing flummoxed. Or seeming to stumble over your words due to overwhelming feelings of nervousness.

From the start, they will judge your character on several things such as:

- How you look.
- How you speak.
- What you say.
- Your body language.
- Your attitude.
- Bring a great attitude. People will forget what you say, but not how you made them feel.
- Greet the interviewer with a smile. A smile can help to build crucial rapport.
- Try to maintain eye contact.
- Be enthusiastic, upbeat, and friendly. People buy people.
- Turn off your phone or put it on silent.
- Do not answer your phone during the interview.
- Shake hands firmly, but don't try to break anyone's bones. It gives the wrong first impression.
- Accept a glass of water if offered. Your mouth may go dry when feeling under pressure.
- Be organised, bring a notepad, pen, and your foundation documents in case they ask.
- Dress the part. Look smart. If unsure, call ahead and ask what is the normal work attire?
- It only takes a few seconds to make a first impression. Aim to look conservative and professional.

- No overbearing perfume or aftershave either. It can be off-putting.
- Allow the interviewer to take a seat first.
- SMILE! Be enthusiastic, but not overboard.
- Try to take a few deep breaths before going into the interview to help you feel calmer.
- If you have done your homework, you will feel confident when answering any curly questions.
- Thank the Interviewer.
- Prepare some answers for any questions you think you may get asked on a pad and look over them whilst waiting for the Interviewer to arrive. It will refresh your memory on critical points you want to make.

Tip 50

BE COMFORTABLE SELLING YOUR SKILLS

Selling yourself is a big part of finding employment. Learning how to explain why you are a great candidate to an employer can take practice. But it's an exercise worth completing.

You might be equally qualified and as experienced as the other applicants. Or even less so. However, if you can describe your skills better, and communicate why your credentials could bring more value to an employer, you will have learnt how to differentiate yourself from the crowd. Thus, potentially giving yourself a greater chance of being selected as the candidate of choice.

Here are a few ideas to help along the way.

- Learn to market yourself, your skills, achievements, career or school successes and experiences.
- An Interviewer will ask you why you are looking for new employment. Have an answer prepared.
- You must know your goals, both long and short-term. They'll want to hear about career aspirations.

- They will probably ask you about the work you're looking for: Part-time, Casual or Permanent?
- Be able to clarify any recent training, workplace skills or experiences, especially if it relates to the job you are applying for.
- Know your skills and learn what an accomplishment or achievement looks like in your chosen occupation.
- Demonstrate how you can motivate and work within a team or independently.
- Determine how much you want to earn, learn to communicate the amount confidently. You will probably get asked.
- Describe that you have the capacity to deliver the results your potential employer is looking for.
- Explain how you can manage different tasks and responsibilities within the job, handle pressure or meet deadlines.
- Illustrate through examples how you can respond to problems and challenges at work. (CAR)
- Most importantly, talk about what you have to offer above anyone else—your value proposition.
- If asked, "Why should we employ you?" Have an answer ready. Be positive, confident and describe how you intend to be successful and what you can bring.

Tip 51

COMMON INTERVIEW Q AND A'S

Q. **What do you know about the position?**
A. Explain a great deal and express some key points found in your research.

Q. **What do you know about our company?**
A. Demonstrate your research. Shine, shine, shine!

Q. **Tell us about yourself.**
A. Don't tell them your life story. Think: Short, sweet and to the point. Be enthusiastic and explain a little about your career to date and how it helps you to fit the role. Treat it as a chance to shine.

Q. **Since Covid, there have been many workplace changes. What have you done to continue to be productive during this time?**
A. Talk about how working from home has allowed you to become even more organised, and technology proficient. Think Zoom, Skype, Microsoft Teams etc.

Q. **What are your strengths?**
A. Think about what the position asks for and focus on those key areas to describe your strengths.

Q. **What are your weaknesses?**
A. Turn the word weakness around in your mind to 'area of development.' Then draw on an answer that wouldn't be a deal breaker for the job. E.g. Need to develop IT skills to a more advanced level.

Q. **Can you give us an example of when you were proactive?**
A. Explain you're naturally self-motivated, then provide an example of when you took your own initiative to undertake a task at work.

Q. **Describe a time when you had to manage your time effectively?**
A. Talk about when you had to meet a tight deadline or juggle priorities to get the job done.

Q. **Why did you leave your last role?**
A. Always lead with a positive answer. Never be negative about an ex-employer. Talk about wanting further growth, or development, or learning opportunities.

Q. **What motivated you to apply for the job?**
A. Here's your chance to shine with the research you have undertaken. Weave it into your answer. Tell them about their own company and how you like the idea they are getting bigger, or more innovative, or leading the way in something, or the service they provide for others, etc.

Q. **What are your career aspirations?**

A. Becoming an expert in your field, assuming a leadership position, earning a degree or certificate.

Q. **When are you available to start?**

A. Immediately!

Tip 52

QUESTIONS TO ASK AT THE INTERVIEW

It is better to have plenty of questions readily available to ask during the interview. It shows you are keen to learn more about the job, the company and your eagerness to join the team.

- Why has the position become available?
- What do you perceive as the main challenging areas?
- What is great about working here?
- Who would I report to?
- Will there be any kind of handover or initial training period?
- Are there any form of flexible work arrangements (think virtual or part-time options)?
- How will my performance be measured?
- What aspects of the role require immediate attention?
- Are there future training or development opportunities?
- How has the business managed the challenges of Covid?
- When is the position likely to start?

Tip 53

DESCRIBE YOUR ACHIEVEMENTS

A key component to being successful at an interview is to know your strengths and accomplishments.

Prepare an extensive list of your achievements. Think about:

- Accolades you have won.
- Successful projects you have managed or been a part of.
- Include problems you have overcome or issues you have addressed.
- Challenges you have faced where your actions led to a positive resolution.
- Value you have added to your team, department or overall company. Include data or statistics.
- "As a result of reviewing our stationery suppliers, I reduced our supplier list from three to one, allowing me to negotiate more favourable prices and reducing costs by 33%."

Think about any challenges or issues you have addressed prior to the interview and conduct some brainstorming exercises by jotting previous experiences down to help you recall the information more quickly.

For example, if the job advert asks for collaboration, organisational skills and negotiation skills as required competencies, then prepare examples of when you have displayed these skills in a previous role.

Younger job seekers may not have a great deal of work experience to draw from. Therefore, it is wholly acceptable to take into account other areas of your life such as school, university, sport, community activities, projects or groups you are part of and use them as examples.

Tip 54

FAKE IT 'TIL YOU MAKE IT

Confidence can be a tricky thing to exude if you are not naturally a confident person. Sometimes we just have to fake it. This means acting in a certain way, the way you want people to perceive you as being. In this case, depicting an image that aligns with what the employer is looking for, which is a self-assured, confident, knowledgeable candidate who is enthusiastic and a good match for the job.

'Faking it' is all about trying to display confidence (when honestly, you don't feel very confident or comfortable in interviews at all). But that's O.K.

What I'm talking about is showing an employer you have what it takes to be the candidate of choice by demonstrating self-assurance and self-belief. Allowing others to believe you have what it takes to be considered as a worthy candidate for the position you have in your sights.

Here's one confidence trick you can learn for yourself to help build your confidence levels: **The Power Pose.**

If you haven't seen this Ted Talk already, please view it in full. Not the short version, the full one. I have shared the link below, but it will take a few seconds to find it on YouTube.

There is a famous talk by Social Psychologist, Amy Cuddy, describing how changing your body posture and physiology can potentially change your levels of confidence before attending an interview. People have viewed it over forty-six million times.

She suggests our body language determines how we think and feel about ourselves, and thus, how we hold our bodies can have a greater impact on our minds. By commanding a powerful stance, we can make ourselves feel more powerful. The evidence of power posing came from a study Cuddy completed while at Harvard University, where participants sat in either a high-power pose (expansive posture) or low-power pose (leaning inward, legs crossed) for two minutes. Cuddy found those who sat in the high-power pose felt more powerful and performed better in mock interviews than those who had not.

It's important to understand Cuddy's research contained two major findings. The first was that people who sat in high-power positions felt more powerful than their low-power pose counterparts. The second was the power posing changed their body chemistry. Amy Cuddy's study suggested those who adopted high-power poses demonstrated an increase in testosterone and a decrease in cortisol. Cuddy interpreted these hormonal effects as further evidence of increases in feelings of power.

After she released her TED talk, it seemed everyone was power posing. Before interviews, job candidates would escape to the toilet to engage in two minutes of high-power posing before meeting their interviewer. Here in Australia, they teach this stuff in some schools.

- Power Posing before an interview entails standing with your hands on your hips, legs apart, standing tall and looking straight ahead.
- Ladies, you will mimic Wonder Woman. Yes, you read that right.
- Guys, standing tall, hands on your hips, legs apart, looking straight ahead. You will mimic Superman. Yep, you read that right too.

What I am sharing is a cool tip for feeling more confident before you walk in for that crucial job interview. The idea and the science behind all this stuff is aimed at helping you perform better.

The Power Pose has been scientifically proven that by changing your shape and adopting a 'predator' pose instead of the 'prey' pose, you are more likely to succeed because you feel so much more confident.

A 'Predator' in the wild will big themselves up, ready to go into battle. Think, Lion, Gorilla, Baboon.

The 'Prey' however will do everything to hide, scurry away and avoid being seen.

Like the way you might feel when you get nervous and wish wholeheartedly you won't get picked to stand up at the front of the room and share your presentation with the team, if you know what I mean. You would just rather not do it.

My honest opinion is this. If you mimic the 'Power Pose' moments before your interview and you feel it gives you a competitive advantage, then why not do it? Standing in front of a mirror for two minutes emulating Wonder Woman or Superman can't be that bad, surely? Additionally, if you get a job offer because your confidence is at an all-time high and you smash it, happy days!

Well, I know I have practised it many times with my clients and we have even had fun performing the pose in groups, and in one-to-one sessions before interviews have taken place. Has it worked? Well, many of my clients said it made them feel more in control. So, I'll take that.

https://www.ted.com/talks/amy_cuddy_your_body_language_may_shape_who_you_are?language=en

The Law of Attraction has a similar movement described as *"Act as if you already have it."*

I'm not talking about power posing here. This is more about believing something is yours and emulating that feeling.

In this case, acting as though the job is already yours. Acting and feeling the way you would if you'd already accomplished the desired outcome.

When speaking to the employer, imagine you're already the employee. Why? Because it will make you sound more confident, feel under less pressure, and enhance your performance. You are trying to show an employer you can add value to their business. It's easier to communicate your 'pitch' when you feel good about yourself.

It's about having faith in your own abilities and believing you can achieve anything you set your mind to. So, think like you can, because honestly, once you think like that, what you can truly achieve will surprise you. I've seen job seekers literally turn their lives around for the better by implementing the same technique. It can, and probably will, have a greater impact on your results.

Tip 55

BE KIND TO YOURSELF

We have covered a lot of ground so far. But I believe this tip plays a crucial part in the success of your job searching efforts.

Remember, I want you to be successful or become even more successful in your quest for employment.

One vital strategy I have learnt over my thirty plus year career history, which has proven to be successful on a regular basis, in both business and in my personal life, is shared below.

It's also the single most important piece of information I can share with you throughout the entire book. Honestly, **Be kind to yourself.**

What? I can hear you exclaim! What are you banging on about, Aly? I bought this book to learn about how to find a job, not listen to your departing pearls of wisdom on becoming a kindness guru!

Yes, yes, yes! Just bear with me, please. If it wasn't relevant or important, then I wouldn't feel the need to share. But I do, so there's method in my madness (as the saying goes).

By applying this super important, yet tiny key piece of advice, it can and probably will make the world of difference between remaining motivated, focused, and positive when you're looking for a job. Alternatively, if not adhered to, it can make the process appear difficult, an uphill struggle and at times, almost unbearable. In fact, an unpleasant experience. One you'd rather avoid at all costs. I cannot overstate how extremely vital it is to follow this instruction. **Be kind to yourself!**

Before you even think about how and where to look for a job, you must try to remember to be kind to yourself during the whole process. Especially, if you want to stay on track and increase your chances of any kind of success. Think about keeping your eyes on the prize. Remain focused on what is important and remove any negative self-talk or as I call it 'self-chatter.'

Start immediately! Treat yourself with the respect you deserve. You are doing the best you can with what God has given you. Tell yourself as often as you possibly can:

"I'm doing my best and my best is enough to progress."

Pull out a post-it note or a piece of paper. Write the above quote out in BIG, CLEAR letters so it's easily visible. Then put it somewhere you can see it and read it every day to help remind yourself that you're doing a great job already. Seeing it will alleviate some of the pressure you are putting on yourself (which is an easy thing to do when you need to earn money). On your wall. Near your laptop, or write it on your mirror, whichever, stick it to your desk. Reiterate it to yourself every day until you accomplish whatever form of employment you have set out to achieve.

When you are at home, applying for jobs by yourself, it's easy to get stuck 'inside your own head.' Applying for job after job can become laborious and frustrating if you are not experiencing any immediate positive results. Reading a positive affirmation daily will help to put things into perspective.

Just do your best. No one expects more than that from you.

We all act differently when we are under pressure. Therefore, if you release some of that pressure by feeding your subconscious mind with positive thoughts, you're more likely to progress the way you intend to.

Sir Richard Branson – Mr. Virgin - Billionaire Tycoon once said:

"If you fall flat on your face, at least you're moving forward. All you have to do is get back up and try again."

I love this saying. After starting my own business, I looked at this quote weekly to keep myself motivated. Because, inevitably, I made some big old stuff ups. However, being kind to myself and 'cutting myself a little slack' now and again allowed me to put it all into perspective and not be as hard on myself for any errors I made. After all, I was still in the early stages of learning how to set up a business. We are all hard on ourselves sometimes. Each of us can be our own worst and hardest Taskmasters.

We all make stuff ups.

You will see a marked improvement in your results when you release some of that pressure, and just go for it (ensuring a quality approach too, may I add).

Freddie Mercury (lead singer of Queen, and my all-time favourite band) famously once said:

"Kind thoughts, kind words, kind deeds."

Being kind to yourself brings higher feelings of positivity. Elevated feelings of positivity will build your levels of confidence whether it's little by little or huge waves of self-confidence. Feeling good about your own efforts can spur you on to achieve things you may never have imagined.

Are you familiar with the term '*Success Breeds Success?*'

It means, the more successful you become at something, the more you seem to magnetise additional success towards you. How does that affect you during job searching? Initial success may be sufficient to trigger a self-propelling cascade of success.

Recently, I worked with a young mum who initially felt completely fed up, disheartened, and demotivated by her job searching results to date. It was obvious to me she had 'gotten inside her own head' with the not-so positive self-chatter because of the way she was describing herself to me. This always makes me want to reach out and help.

Within a few weeks, we worked together identifying possible reasons her applications were being unsuccessful (effectively, she was overloading the applications with far too much irrelevant information. She was then talking herself out of opportunities because she didn't have anyone to bounce her 'pitch' off). After we stripped it all back to basics, and identified her strengths and key skills, her successes seemed to build. Reaching a point after six weeks of partnering together for one hour per week, she received multiple job offers and she almost couldn't decide which one to take.

Eventually, she decided upon one and loved being back in the workplace. Literally, it seemed to be the more positive she felt toward the process, the better she became at it. She was honing her skills along the way. Her successes were gathering momentum.

Whatever happens when you begin looking for employment, make sure you speak to yourself in a kind way, with kind words. (And we all talk to ourselves, so don't pretend you don't).

What I have learnt from watching many people succeed and sadly, why several people fail is this. When you learn to be positive about yourself, and be kind to yourself regarding your own efforts, you will feel good most of the time about the progress you're making and the jobs you're applying for. It's an attitude of enthusiasm and it will come through in your job applications.

It's inevitable you have more faith in yourself, faith in your own abilities and faith that an employer is likely to get back to you soon.

Start today by eliminating the urge to say disparaging comments to yourself. Avoid criticising yourself at any cost. Replace any negatives with kinder thoughts and deeds to help you progress. You've got this! Remind yourself, you are doing O.K. Even after making lots of phone calls, sending out what seems to be a never-ending stream of emails, building connections or making numerous job applications. Just remember, it's a process. A process which entails not beating yourself up at every chance when things don't pan out the way you first imagined.

Maybe you're not experiencing any signs of early success. But you will. I'm certain. You must look after your mental attitude. Look in the mirror and start 'bigging yourself up.' Give yourself a break. Think positively about what you could achieve and what the fruits of your labour might bring. A new suit, dress, trainers, weekend away, Botox, wine, holidays, cars, financial stability… Whatever your thing is, keep the end goal in mind to remain focused.

Reassure yourself that it will all be worthwhile when you see the progress you have made. Kindness is key! Keeping your chin up, even if you have received the odd rejection letter, will allow you to continue in the direction you're aiming towards.

I have faith in you and your abilities.

Tip 56

REMOVE THE NEGATIVE SELF-CHATTER

Closely monitoring what you say to yourself is super important from day dot. Check out the psychology research for further evidence in case you want additional confirmation. When an individual loses their job, it has an immediate impact on the way they can feel.

It is essential to look after your own mental health throughout this process.

Norman Vincent Peel wrote a famous book entitled the *'Power of Positivity Thinking'* selling around five million copies. One of my favourite quotes is:

"Change your thoughts and you change the world."

What a remarkable man! What a remarkable idea!

Research proves we become less successful at finding creative solutions for problems when we allow ourselves to focus inwards, on the negativity, resulting in others doubting us too. Or in this case, we doubt our own abilities to undertake the tasks in front of us. We procrastinate and put things off, avoiding the whole job-hunting process altogether.

At worst, if we doubt ourselves, and can't communicate our value to an employer, how can we expect the employer to see the value we bring? That's why it's imperative to banish all doubt from the start. Believe you've got this! Others will then follow your lead.

Think about it. If you don't believe in your abilities, how do you expect an employer to? Help an employer believe in you.

Another famous quote from the *'Power of Positivity Thinking'* is:

"Believe and Succeed."

I am lucky. I am a positive, self-assured, confident person. But my confidence has developed over time. It is a skill I have worked on and honed over the years. Now I help my clients to recognise their expertise, which builds confidence, and they sing it from the rooftops because if they don't, who else will?

You can learn to do the same. Start by focussing on the positive elements of what you can do and what you are good at. Think about your strengths. Recognise your unique selling points and remind yourself daily that you are in a bridging phase of your career. You're on your way to finding or changing your job, embarking on a new part of the career journey or establishing a new career entirely.

Correcting your self-talk when it's unconstructive can keep you focused and help to boost your self-esteem, therefore, promoting self-confidence. Appearing self-confident is important when you're trying to find a job. Why? Because when you are feeling confident, you communicate more clearly. In particular, when talking to potential employers and discussing your skills, strengths, qualifications, experience, and abilities, the employer will automatically hear the confidence in your voice. I know because I have conducted literally thousands of phone interviews and phone screens in my time.

An interviewer can instantly tell when someone seems positive, keen and able to communicate their abilities confidently, because the conversation runs more smoothly. There are less uncomfortable silences.

The job seeker answers questions with an air of assurance, sounding upbeat and optimistic, giving the prospective employer greater confidence in their own hiring decision.

Alternatively, if you allow the self-chatter to continue and be negative, overwhelming feelings of frustration can and probably will take over, turning optimistic thoughts into doubtful ones instead. This results in lower levels of self-confidence, making you feel like the process is far too much like hard work and eventually giving up.

Getting ***Your Rear into Gear*** is all about helping you to learn how to play the job-hunting game. You now have the opportunity to learn how to put your 'Game Face' on (a facial expression that suggests a strong determination to succeed). We all have a 'Game Face' whether it be at school, work, sport, exercise, in the pub, at home or with the with the in-laws. It's about turning up the energy when you need to, even if you don't always feel like it. Once you find a job, or change careers, you will feel a huge sense of accomplishment.

Keep feeding your mental platter positive constructive thoughts to help keep you motivated and on track. Eventually, you'll propel yourself forward and ultimately progress towards where you want to be.

Tip 57

REWARD YOUR EFFORTS

Occasionally, reward yourself for your hard work. Whether that means taking a break, grabbing a cuppa, popping out for some fresh air, meeting a friend for lunch. Making friends with the biscuit tin (as I do far too often). Or congratulating yourself for your efforts and your tenacious approach.

Only you can measure your success. Everyone's idea of success is different too. What success looks like for one person, often looks completely different to another. Here's an example.

Securing a part-time job within school hours, five days a week, could be a huge win if you're a mum re-entering the workforce after establishing a family (something I have done myself). Those jobs are rare gems and precious opportunities not to be missed. So, finding paid employment, in a job you enjoy, to fit around your family and your kids is HUGE! Remind yourself just what a BIG DEAL that really is. You've done great!

- During the job-hunting process, consider treating yourself to a small reward for your early wins.

- At the end of your first week, and every week thereafter of 'knuckling down,' maybe grab a personal treat; a bottle of wine or some gorgeous bath salts for a relaxing bath when the kids are in bed.
- Possibly get your nails done, maybe a pedicure, facial or new haircut.
- Treat yourself to something that continues to make you feel good.
- Maybe hit up the iTunes, visit your favourite burger bar, buy a new T-shirt or take time out for yourself to go to the gym, have a massage or watch your favourite sport.
- Think about buying a new book or treating yourself to a beer or wine with lunch.
- Whatever makes you feel great! Just do something that feels like you have given yourself a reward for your toil.
- When you head into the next week, feeling more inspired, and good about your achievements to date, you are more likely to continue until you reach a new benchmark or milestone.
- It's all about progress. It could be an offer of casual work as a stepping stone job. A fill-in role. Temporary work that could turn into a longer-term contract. A chance to volunteer with a community organisation to build your skills in a particular area or build your confidence before returning to work on a full-time basis. Voluntary work has so many benefits. Giving something back to your community comes with a great feel-good factor. And it doesn't have to be forty hours a week. Maybe read with children at your local primary school for a few hours a week.

- We all have skills we can share, and it helps to build our confidence and networks into the bargain.

Rewarding yourself for achieving some small initial goals doesn't have to cost a fortune either. My treat is always a packet of Rolos and a coffee. I love Rolos!

What I'm saying is, look out for the small wins regardless of how insignificant they may seem on the surface. You need to recognise progress when you see it.

There are squillions of reasons to celebrate small wins or huge feats (yes, squillions, another oh-so professional term). Above all, the small steps help you gain momentum towards the bigger goals, and ultimately reaching your desired outcome. In this scenario, it's the job offer you really want.

If you don't believe me, or think this is mumbo jumbo, here's what Tony Robbins, Number 1 Motivational Coach on the planet says about rewarding yourself.

"It's important to reward yourself, and your team as soon as you complete a key task or objective. Why? By rewarding yourself in the moment, your brain elicits positive emotions, leading to the realisation that your efforts result in a positive reward. By doing this continuously, your brain will start to link pleasure to accomplishing the task or objective and move towards it in the future."

As Tony says, "You can only build on success!"

Whatever your circumstances, you should apply the same methods. Recognise your own efforts. Reward yourself for trying.

Tip 58

RINSE AND REPEAT METHOD

In an earlier tip, I shared the importance of having your foundation documents ready to go. An extra advantage to having all of your foundation documents prepared in advance comes when you create multiple job applications. Applying the 'rinse and repeat' method is a great way to increase the quantity of job applications without compromising on the quality of your documentation. This allows you to contact more employers without having to go back to the 'drawing board' every time.

- 'Rinse and repeat' is an effective technique that allows you to produce an increased volume of applications over a shorter space of time, thus increasing your chances of success.
- The more quality job applications you make, the more likely you are to hear from an employer.
- Employers need to know you are available, so you have to tell as many as possible. They will not come to you if they don't know you're out there.

- Remember to tweak your 'Professional Profile' for every job you are applying for. Tailor it to meet the needs of the employer. This should not take you long.
- Include keywords from the job description where possible to beat the ATS.
- Have a good foundation Cover Letter ready to amend accordingly, addressing the selection criteria.

Example of what not to do:

- BEWARE! Do not just fire off random job applications without first checking the content of your resume or cover letter.
- There is nothing worse that receiving a cover letter addressed to the wrong person. It goes straight in the 'No' pile.
- Recruiters and hiring managers are looking for an excuse to short-list applicants.
- Demonstrating to an employer you have taken care and paid attention to the required details in the job advert and addressed the essential criteria will pay dividends.
- It's important to show the employer you want to be taken seriously; you are capable of meeting their expectations by communicating effectively in writing.
- It also proves you are thorough and have considered all the elements requiring high attention to detail from the very beginning.

Above all, ensure your application looks as though you have tailored it to meet their specific needs. No one wants another generic application you have zipped off to yet another employer with a bog-standard resume and cover letter without having deliberated first what the employer might expect from your application.

Tip 59

ATTITUDE – PICK A GOOD ONE

This point is worth mentioning more than once.

A great attitude means everything when we're talking job searching.

- It helps us start with a sense of great anticipation, expecting good results.
- Whatever you feel about interviews, having a positive attitude on the day might land you a job offer.
- It makes a big difference in demonstrating your enthusiasm and motivation for the position which assists the interviewer to form a positive opinion of you.
- Turning up to an interview with a bad attitude only encourages a Hiring Manager to decline you.
- Negative attitudes can give the impression of underperformance, appearing ill-prepared, disinterested, anxious or unenthusiastic.
- Show an employer your high levels of interest towards working in their business.

- Outshine the competition by helping the interviewer remember you because of your upbeat, professional attitude.
- Make it difficult for the Hiring Manager to want to choose any other candidate than you.
- Looking professional and sounding professional demonstrates you want to be taken seriously.
- Standing with a great posture, head held high communicates a positive attitude through your body language, showing you're interested and happy to be there.
- A great attitude entices an employer to want to get you on board in their business.
- A great attitude influences all of our actions.
- A great attitude provides better results.
- Employers choose the job applicant they like, often basing their decision on a person's attitude rather than level of experience.

Tip 60

FAITH, COURAGE AND DISCIPLINE

It's time to touch on the subject of being proactive and keeping oneself motivated along with how it's going to help you in the long-term. There are three words written on the wall in my office, just above my laptop (along with the photos of my family and my vision board). These three words keep me on track every day. They keep my levels of motivation where they need to be, so I can serve others to the best of my ability as a Career Coach.

It becomes easier to keep others inspired and equally motivated when I'm feeling energised, upbeat, positive and hungry for success. Which assists them in creating the results they need to reach their goals and achieve their successful outcomes.

To be successful when applying for a job in a crowded market, or tapping into the hidden job market, or to keep your job searching strategies in check, you will need a hefty dollop of each of these things.

- **Faith** in yourself, that you have what it takes to pull this task off.
- Faith you can be successful even after experiencing a few knock backs.
- Faith in what you are aiming to achieve will happen sooner or later. Especially when it feels tough.
- Faith in an employer. That they will recognise the value you bring to their business.
- **Confidence** in your own abilities.
- Confidence to contact employers, knowing you might experience rejection more than once before becoming successful.
- Confidence knowing your efforts will be rewarded no matter how many times you try.
- Confidence the advantages of embarking on this path will far outweigh the disadvantages.
- Confidence knowing you will pull off a great interview and be the candidate of choice.
- **Discipline** in yourself to knuckle down and get the job done.
- Discipline to stay on track, measuring your results, doubling down on your efforts, and remaining focused regardless of the surrounding distractions.
- **Self-discipline** to ensure you allocate time every day to make the calls.
- Self-discipline to stick to the career plan.
- Self-discipline to undertake tasks even when you don't feel like it. That's what makes a champion.
- Self-discipline to send the emails and follow up every lead.

Napoleon Hill, known today as the Godfather of motivational speakers, recognised the value of faith and optimism. He understood all too well what one individual could achieve if they put their mind to it.

If an individual, just like you or me, backed themselves from the start, the process could create almost unimaginable results for that person. It wouldn't matter which field of business or occupation they chose; they would succeed with a true sense of optimism and unwavering faith. He understood the success a person could achieve if that individual acted with a real sense of expectation and maintained a high level of self-belief and motivation throughout their journey.

His book '*Think and Grow Rich*' has sold over ten million copies worldwide. It's a book I would highly recommend to anyone who needs direction, clarity and additional motivation during their career journey. He spent twenty-five years researching the content, interviewing influential figures and documenting details about how to be successful. The book was first published in the 1930s.

Now you are probably thinking, what does a motivational speaker from the 1930s have to do with the hidden job market and my job searching efforts? Well, everything. Because he, like many others since then, such as Jim Rohan, Bob Proctor, Tony Robbins, Bill Gates, Steve Jobs, Les Brown, Oprah Winfrey and Hal Elrod recognised the power of self-belief.

I have an unwavering desire to help as many job seekers on this planet to find employment by sharing as much knowledge and experience as I can. Especially because I truly believe it will help to progress your job searching strategy one step closer, eventually giving you a better chance to find a position of your choosing.

Here I would like to highlight how you stand a greater chance of securing the job you're aiming for.

***"Try not to become a man of success, but rather try to become a man of value.*"** Albert Einstein

If you learn to implement this straightforward strategy, you will set yourself apart from your competitors. They are the other applicants who want to be considered for the roles you are applying for.

By going the extra mile, whether it's volunteer or paid work, by showing a 'can do, will do attitude', you will eventually win the day. You'll have demonstrated how you can be of greater value than the other candidates because of your diligent approach, professional attitude, self-confidence, proven abilities and above all willingness to do what it takes.

Employers want prospective employees to be the solution to the problem. That means they are expecting you to bring something extra to the role, hence 'adding value'.

Once you shift your focus from trying to get a job to wanting to help the employer be more successful, then you will not just be meeting an employer's expectations, but exceeding them. See the opportunity as a way of adding something to their business.

Another quote you will probably be familiar with by Confucius is this.

"Choose a job you love, and you will never have to work a day in your life."

The same principle applies to you. Aim to find a job you will really enjoy as the outcome of your desire. The self-test on whether you love the job is simple: Would you undertake the responsibilities even if you didn't get paid for it? (Or even consider staying late to work overtime just because you're not in it for the money?) If the answer is yes, then you are probably in the right position.

Previously, I mentioned this quote, although I feel it is important to reiterate it.

"The greatest gift you could ever give to another is your highest expectation of their success!"

I have no doubt in my mind that you can and will be successful.

I truly believe you have what it takes to achieve whatever form of employment goal you set yourself to accomplish. We all need a little direction at times, so I hope you have found the content here beneficial, and it has given you several tips you had not considered before and inspired you to take action. If you believe some or many of the tips throughout the book to be helpful, kindly share the tips with others who could benefit. Or tell them the name of the book and where to buy a copy for others to propel their job searching journey forwards and find a fulfilling and rewarding job.

www.alisonbannister.com

I will leave you with one final quote from Les Brown, US Motivational Speaker.

"You do not have to be great to get started, but you do have to get started to be great."

I genuinely wish you every success and hope you feel more inspired to ***Get Your Rear into Gear*** today.

Love

Aly x

TESTIMONIALS

Isabella S – *Mature Aged Job Seeker/Workshop participant*
I find Alison Bannister a very informative, caring Career Coach, who truly gives 110%, in person and online. I have attended her workshops and have always felt motivated, encouraged and hopeful. I highly recommend anyone looking for work and needing professional guidance, to book into a workshop with her. Thank you, Alison, for your help and support, but most of all for being so inspirational.

Charmaine P – *Library Officer WA Local Government*
Alison was a fantastic mentor and coach to me in my search to find new employment after my role was made redundant at the end of 2019. Her knowledge is second to none. She overhauled my resume and cover letter which then resulted in me getting to the interview stage. She coached me on interview techniques. She buoyed up my morale when I had some disappointing rejections. She encouraged me and made me feel valued.

Honestly Alison I am most grateful to you and know that I would not have been able to get the position I now have without you. You are truly worth your weight in gold. I absolutely cannot thank you enough. If anyone is thinking of enlisting Alison's services then you will be making a great investment in yourself and your life that will get the result of securing a job.

Claire T – *Program Manager WA Local Government*
Aly is a true professional and gives you 110% of her knowledge, time and commitment. Her enthusiasm is sure to get you motivated and on your journey. I wouldn't hesitate to recommend the services of Alison Bannister Career Coaching.

David V – *Mature Job Seeker*
Very professional. Alison guided me to relevant contacts to pursue my next career aims and showed me how to make my resume stand out.

Will highly recommend.

Alice T – *Medical Secretary*
Returning to the workforce after taking time to focus on other aspects of someone's life can be daunting. Alison is very approachable and helped update my resume and I have learnt new skills when applying for jobs. She gave me valuable coaching for interviews. Her support has helped me develop further job hunting skills and my confidence.

Kristina B – *Childcare Manager*
Alison really helped me gain confidence to get back into the workforce after being on Maternity leave for eleven months. After just one webinar, her personality just clicked with me and I felt confident with her helping me with my journey. Thank you so much for all the encouragement.

Camilla C – *Customer Service Team Leader*
Alison was incredibly helpful. As well as giving practical advice and strategies, she helped build my confidence after a stressful move across the state.

I wouldn't hesitate to recommend her to anyone looking for help or guidance with their career or job search.

Nuala F – *Learning and Development Manager, WA Government.*
I chose to work with Alison after researching MANY career coaches. I loved her down to earth approach and that she understood the fear of venturing out of my comfort zone. I recently posted to WA from interstate with my partner and was lost as to how to start all over again. Working with Aly has given me a range of tools to make the job search less daunting and her extensive experience is a God send. She is not only helpful with documents like resumes, etc but she helps you see your worth and the fantastic range of skills you have to offer. She has made this journey an enjoyable one and helped me gain the confidence to apply successfully for positions I previously felt were out of reach.

Matt P – *Cultural Leader, Friend and Ex-Colleague*
Aly is a fantastic human being! She is giving, caring, funny, supportive and helps to draw the best out of you, to share and show, who you truly can be and become! I have known and worked with Aly over many years and have no issues in endorsing her character, professionalism, skill and ultimately, her care for the work that she does, that she delivers and provides to those fortunate to learn and share alongside her! Awesome Aly - keep up the great work!

Tracy W – *Museum Guide*
Great news! I've been selected to do a video assessment for the position at the museum that you helped me with.

Thanks so much, you've been a huge help and I really, really appreciate you taking the time to give me feedback. I know how busy you must be so I'm very grateful and it's made my application sound so much better.

Jessica F – *Career Workshop participant*
Thank you for hosting the webinar 'Job Searching in the Current Climate.' I feel you passed on some helpful information to set off on a practical job search at this time and am filled with confidence in how to improve the quality of me and my skills as an employee. I am now working on my Job Seeker Profiles! Thank you.

Davinder K – *Nursing Assistant*
Alison is amazing person and very professional in her work. She helped me a lot in my job search journey. I highly recommend her. Thank you very much Alison for your help.

Denise M – *Virtual Executive Assistant*
Awesome Resume Workshop course, great information, tips and advice all laid out in a easy to understand format which gave a clear idea of what to do and what not to do in updating my resume. Alison is very professional, has an obvious passion for the industry and an eagerness to genuinely help people. Would definitely recommend attending her workshops or webinars. Thanks Alison!

Donna B – *CEO and Business Strategist*
I work with many Defence partners who are looking to start a new business or change careers, and I automatically send them to Aly to discuss their options, learn about how to transition to a new career, or even to write a new resume. Aly is superb!

Ripeka H – *Program Manager, Local Government*
Alison is an excellent career coach! She's an absolute expert in her field. She's an amazing presenter full of energy and enthusiasm,

very inspiring and extremely knowledgeable. Thanks for your awesomeness, Alison!

Lilly M – *Career Workshop Participant*
I attended two of Alison's workshops at the library and was filled with hope and enthusiasm. Job hunting can be a soul-destroying time in your life but Alison's passion shines through the gloom and makes you feel ready to tackle that gruelling selection criteria again. I highly recommend Alison's services.

Aimee S – *Psychology Graduate and Mental Health Advocate*
Alison Bannister was amazingly helpful. She helped me gain the skills and confidence necessary to obtain a job. She is extremely personable and always eager to help with everything from social media to interviews to moral support. If you need help with employment, I highly recommend Alison!

Char-Lee C – *Luxury Travel Tour Manager*
Aly has been incredibly supportive and motivating throughout my transition back into professional life from becoming a mum.

Along with tailoring my resume, editing cover letters and drafting selection criteria, she has been a positive presence and confidence booster.

I highly recommend her services for ADF partners looking to get back into the workforce from motherhood or transferring interstate.

Jo R – *Teacher Special Needs*
Not your everyday career coach.

Alison not only delivers plenty of useful information and key tips for jobseekers, she also goes the extra mile.

After the course, she will email you her presentation, template resumes and cover letters, plus extra links to helpful online services and information. Alison keeps her presentation on track whilst actively engaging with class participants. It's obvious she is passionate about helping others. Personally, I found her two courses motivating. Like all good teachers, Alison won't do the work for you, but she will provide you with all the tools you need to be successful in getting to the next level.

Victoria D – *Secretariat/Executive Officer*
Working with Alison is inspiring. Her experience and knowledge are exceptional, and I felt comfortable and totally assured in my decision to seek her services. I've learned a lot about the job search process, and she has increased my confidence immeasurably. 100% recommend! 5/5 stars from me. Thank you Aly!

Ian C – *Automotive Service Delivery Manager*
Alison is an extremely knowledgeable instructor who goes out of her way to ensure everyone who participates in her seminars gets the full gambit of her years of experience.

One of Alison's great talents is her ability to make all who attend feel at ease and not afraid to ask questions.

Lauren D – *Chemist*
Alison was extremely encouraging and helpful putting together a resume, cover letter and interview questions for me after a lengthy period out of the workforce. Alison is very professional while being friendly and approachable making it very easy to work with her.

Carol E – *Business Owner and Career Coach*
As a coach and trainer, Aly is engaging and motivated. I benefited

greatly from our goal setting during coaching and found her CV writing course to be informative and helpful.

Michelle P – *RSPCA Trainee*
Alison, thank you so much for helping me with my cover letter to apply for the course I dreamed of doing. With only a few people being selected, with your help, I was able to secure a position.

Thank you for your ongoing help and being so attentive whenever I have emailed you.

The support you provide is beyond words, and I can't thank you enough for the service you provide.

When it comes to resume and cover letter writing it's definitely not my strong point and you have given me the confidence and support to push past my daunting fear of getting back into the workforce or study environment, thank you!

Vic H – *Career Workshop Participant*
Engaging and informative. Thanks for a great session!

Melissa R – *Child Residential Support Worker*
Aly has really helped me with my resume and my confidence in finding work. I highly recommend her!

Des – *Youth Worker*
Very informative and gained quite a bit of very useful knowledge.

Stephen T – *Website Designer and Business Owner*
It's always a pleasure working with Alison. We were privileged to be chosen to develop and manage Alison's websites, Alison is very knowledgeable and provides her clients with invaluable information to enable them to land their dream job. All the best, Aly.

Renae H – *Tax Accountant and New Business Owner*

Alison (Aly) Bannister would be one of the most motivational, enthusiastic women I have the privilege of working with - and this is evident with just recently awarded second place at 2019 WA Business Awards - AusMumpreneur Awards and third place at 2019 Rockingham Kwinana Chamber of Commerce Peoples' Choice Awards.

Aly provides professional career coaching and guidance and loves helping people change their lives and shape their careers. Her positive, can-do attitude will rub off on you, put you in the right mind-set and get you where you deserve to be!

Leanne B – *Aged Care Support Worker*

I would like to thank the City of Kwinana for offering the Resume Clinics and the Mature Aged Job Seekers Workshop facilitated by Alison Bannister from ABCC.

Alison has a real passion for what she does, and I feel fortunate to have crossed her path. Time spent with Alison has lifted my spirits and given me real hope that I can achieve my goals and get back into the workforce.

I have learnt a lot about writing a Resume, as well as Job Searching tips and some techniques to be successful at interview. I even secured an interview for the first time in two years.

Alison has a professional approach and is very well informed. Her honesty and sense of humour seemed to lighten the workshop energy and make it really enjoyable. She also gave out some great handouts with really useful information.

Sandra T – *PR Specialist*

Alison is absolutely amazing at what she does. One of the best career coaches I've had a consultation with.

Rachel F – *Business Owner*
I want to give you my feedback on the information session I attended this morning with Alison Bannister.

I am thoroughly impressed. Fantastic course content. Alison is an engaging presenter who made an overwhelming and complex subject matter easy to digest and understand. Her material was relevant, her examples highlighted each point wonderfully and she was approachable, pleasant, professional and made complete sense!!!

She clearly knows her audience and subject matter well (having lived it herself), was familiar with speaking to mums who want to be entrepreneurs and is truly passionate about helping others. I have taken many 'learnings' from this morning's course.

Overall, great presentation, user-friendly platform (zoom - there is no way with my current situation I would be able to take the time to travel to a formal location for such a presentation/ info session), insightful information and worthwhile experience. I highly recommend and would sign up to another course run by Alison without hesitation.

Thank you for your communication and for organising this course.

Billy G – *IT Consultant*
I am very grateful for the professional advice received from Alison Bannister Career coaching. I was struggling to effectively apply for new roles after finishing my IT Qualification. Alison helped me to create my Resume and cover letters to look more appealing to my new potential employers. She assisted me in contacting agencies and local businesses. Set weekly goals for me to complete in order to keep up my focused. Thank you so much, Alison, you're a superstar. Billy G .

Testimonials from Australian Defence Force Spouses and Girlfriends

Freya W - *Project Coordinator and Analyst*

Working with Aly from Aly Bannister Career Consulting has been one of the best career choices I have made. As we prepare for our fifth Defence move interstate, she has guided me through what can be an overwhelming process of finding employment in a new city. Adding to this, my wish to enter a new industry post-Master's degree. Her job coaching has provided a thorough approach that encompassed areas such as networking, job searching, resume writing and interview preparation. The skills she has given to me are invaluable and very much appreciated.

Laura-Lee M – *Engineer and Continuous Improvement Manager*

Alison has been a great resource and support for local job searches as well as getting my resume updated. Really appreciate the work she has provided!

Christina P – *Workshop participant and Medical Receptionist*

As a stay-at-home mum who has only been able to work casually for the past few years, Aly helped me to think outside my comfort zone. She showed me how to identify my strengths and the many transferable skills I can offer to employers. Aly is such a positive person; her laughter fills the room making job hunting an enjoyable experience. I look forward to continuing to work with her in the future and cannot recommend her highly enough as a career coach.

Karen R – *Administration Manager and ADF Spouse*
From the moment I engaged Alison Bannister of ABCC to assist with updating my Resume, digital profiles and career choices; I have found Alison to be exceptionally professional and well-prepared for our phone meetings. Aly's knowledge of the recruitment industry but also her willingness to share her knowledge helps to shed light on possibilities! Aly has gone above and beyond for me and I have no qualms in recommending Alison Bannister to help with your next career move.

Andrea D – *Executive Property Manager*
I recently attended a Career workshop with Alison Bannister. I have been searching for a job with very little success, I drew up my own resume and cover letter. At the workshop Aly went through the DO's and DONT'S of a resume and what the employer would be looking at. I had drawn up a resume with just about all of the DONT'S!

One-on-one coaching with Aly has been so informative and, she created different resumes and cover letters for the different jobs for which I had the skills. She showed other platforms where I could look for employment and sent relevant links for more information. We went through the ads which I wanted to apply for, teaching me how to write a great cover letter.

Aly is professional yet caring and creates a safe space, I also found she really helped me understand specifically where and with who I would like to work, thereby creating long term job satisfaction, her attention to detail shows in the quality of her work.

Since working with Aly I have been able to apply for more jobs which suit me and I have much more confidence within the content which I am sending.

I would be happy to answer any questions or have a further chat regarding this service.

Elizabeth P – *Graphic Designer and ADF Spouse*
I highly recommend Alison for anyone seeking Career Coaching, Resume Writing and Interview Preparation.

I didn't even know I needed help until I started speaking with her. She has been instrumental in helping me decide what sort of employment suits me and my personal commitments and how best to apply.

My dream job came up and Alison dropped everything and helped me prepare my resume and cover letter and within twenty-four hours, I had an interview locked in!

Alison understands the demands of juggling motherhood and a career. She is also experienced with the challenges defence families are faced with and how these challenges may affect the job search or job choice.

Alison helped me identify what sort of job I really wanted and how to create/find it. She is amazing and I wouldn't have got this far without her!"

Leanne W – *ADF Spouse and Environmentalist*
I heard Aly speak at RAAF Base Pearce this year and found her motivated and forthright. I have since then applied for Partner Employment Assistance Program with Aly's guidance and am in the process of returning to work, which 6 months ago seemed beyond me. Thank you!

Jane S – *Teacher and ADF Spouse*
To Whom it may concern,

I am writing to recommend Alison Bannister from Career

Coaching for her excellent service provided to me whilst applying for a teaching position last week. I was so impressed by Alison's ability to work above and beyond the time scheduled in the quote in order to provide an excellent application.

Alison's professional, kind and friendly demeanour made the process less stressful. Her reliability and dedication to her job was outstanding. I would be more than happy to recommend Alison to any other client and applaud her for her commitment.

Emily K – *Pearce Community Group Coordinator, RAAF Pearce*
In August 2019, Alison (Aly) came out to Pearce Community Group to run a Hidden Job Market workshop for us. Her professionalism, knowledge and passion for partner employment is fantastic. Her flexibility when working with families is outstanding.

Aly is such an asset to anyone looking for work or upskilling. Her passion and knowledge is incredible and her commitment to you is like no other. Needing career advice/support look no further! Thank you Aly!

Danni I – *Fashion Buyer*
Alison was extremely knowledgeable and up to date with the current job market and her friendly, engaging and approachable manner made the workshop a very positive and enjoyable experience.

Maria Y – *ADF Spouse and Teacher*
Alison Bannister gave me an exceptional service when I was in need of a new resume. I had been out of my profession as a Teacher for some time – having recently completed my family. Therefore, starting my job searching journey and returning to

the workforce was a little daunting to begin with. However, with Alison's creativity and professional guidance I finally had a resume I was proud of that reflected my skills and true capabilities. In fact, within a few weeks of Alison completing my resume, I found work immediately. I would highly recommend her services to any ADF Spouse or Partner who wants a Career Coach that offers encouragement, guidance and support.

Claire G – *Marilla Community Centre Coordinator*
Engaging with Alison Bannister Career Coaching has been such a positive experience for both our community centre and our Australian Defence Force Partner members. Alison has facilitated both paid and free Career workshops to better support ADF Partners into the WA workforce. As a direct result of her commitment, passion and dedication, a number of our members have secured long-term employment. Alison is knowledgeable, professional and is truly committed to helping ADF Partners improve their chances of gaining lasting employment. Alison has also guided many of our participants to the PEAP program, which they may not have otherwise accessed. I would highly recommend her services to any business or individual seeking a professional Career Coaching service.

Lauren D – *ADF Spouse and Quality Control Chemist*
I was lucky enough to be introduced to Alison through the Career Workshops program run through Marilla house. Alison's encouragement, advice and skills have given me the confidence to believe that I can get back into the workforce, even after children and with the uncertainty of defence life.

Kristy B – *Office Administrator*
Just emailing to thank you for holding the Contemporary Job Searching seminar yesterday. It was a great opportunity to listen to your advice and enjoy hearing your work stories too. It was all very relatable and told in a professional but friendly manner. Your sense of humour and non-judgemental manner made for a very enjoyable morning.

Thanks and regards.

Dianne R – *Administrator*
Your encouraging nature and positivity is so refreshing and such a bonus, which helps to keep us motivated with learning and focus during this time. We both look forward to seeing you at your next workshop.

Disability Employment Sector

Jacqui C – *Registered Nurse*
I had the pleasure of meeting Aly in 2016. I was unemployed and had been for two years following a medical condition.

Aly updated and revamped my resume and complied a cover letter. Aly developed a comprehensive and proactive job seeking plan. She assisted me with strategies, on how to apply for a variety of positions. These enabled and empowered me, in reaching my goal of successfully returning to the work force.

Aly's knowledge base and contacts in the employment industry were exemplary.

I am happy to say, I was successful in securing a Permanent Team Lead position in a Community based Organisation.

Aly's commitment to achieving success, her passion in enabling and empowering people, is the reason I have and continue to highly recommend her service to any individual whom is in need of any aspect related to a Career Coaching.

Shirley Van Rosi – *Information Officer, Government of Western Australia*
I met Aly In mid-2016. I had been unemployed for three years due to illness. Aly helped me in determining what career path would be best suited for me and we created a career plan, reviewed and updated my resume, employment portals and she oversaw my applications. Aly's networking contacts got me into an interview, and I landed a departmental contracting position in February 2016 and I am now in a permanent position with the department. Aly was instrumental with her support and encouragement and I would highly recommend her as a Career Coach and a person.

Lindy O – *Travel Manager*
Dear Alison, I can't tell you how lovely it was to meet you today. I walked out feeling 'not so helpless' and I cannot tell you how much that meant to me. Well I'm sure you are well aware lol. I will definitely be asking if there is more information that I can access like this. I will also be giving feedback to the organisation that kindly arranged for you to attend. I would love to meet with you again. Thank you so much for your time and career support.

ABOUT ALY

Aly Bannister is an award-winning Career Coach with hundreds of testimonials testifying to her abilities, passion, and dedication towards helping job seekers find employment.

Now she has combined her depth of knowledge, breadth of experience, skills, and genuine desire to help you, along with one million other Australian job seekers, to find employment and create real and lasting career success.

Aly has been partnering with job seekers for over thirty years (starting out in Recruitment back in 1987. Even before the internet arrived).

Her experience comes from HR, Talent Advice, Disability Employment, Job Active, Prisoner Employment Programs, Community Volunteer Projects and Government Programs. She has assisted thousands of individuals, from all walks of life, to become more successful throughout the job-hunting process. Now, she is sharing her knowledge, tips, and tricks to help you be more successful, achieve greater results and get that all-important job application over the line. Ideally, for you to progress to the interview stage and ultimately be hired.

Aly has gained a reputation for her realistic, motivational approach, authentic and relatable style with a no-nonsense yet caring attitude. In addition, she layers her practical guidance with dollops of passion, and piles of positivity. All the ingredients needed to achieve long-term success. Each element is thrown in to make a real and lasting difference.

The overall aim of this book is to add value to the lives of job seekers all over the country and make a positive impact. One towards changing lives for the better and helping to shape careers.

So, whether you want a job purely to put food on the table, or provide an income for your family, work part-time to fund your studies, pay the bills or reach the pinnacle of your profession and achieve long-lasting career success, look no further. This book can help! It provides information to better prepare you for your job searching journey ahead.

Congratulations! You have just taken the first step in the right direction. And it's called ***Getting Your Rear into Gear!***

So, let's get started straight away.

USEFUL WEBSITES TO CONSIDER IN AUSTRALIA

Job Outlook

- https://joboutlook.gov.au/

Job Outlook is an online guide to careers and trends in the jobs market. It can help you find careers that match your interests, experience or skillset, and has the information you need to make a decision in your job search, study or training pathway. It is a government-funded site.

Jobs Hub Department of Education, Skills and Employment

- https://www.dese.gov.au/

Jobs Hub provides information on current employment opportunities, what's happening in the Australian job market, and jobs that are in demand. While many businesses have been adversely affected by COVID-19 and are reducing their workforces, there are some areas of the economy which have increased demand for workers.

LinkedIn

- www.linkedin.com

LinkedIn is a social network site that focuses on professional networking and career development. You can use LinkedIn to display your resume, search for jobs, and enhance your professional reputation by posting updates and interacting with other people.

Job Jump Start

- https://www.jobjumpstart.gov.au/

Job Jumpstart is a new Government website that enables young people to take control of their job search and career planning. The website offers articles on a vast range of topics, including searching and applying for jobs, networking and personal presentation, and starting a new job.

Ethical Jobs/Care Careers

- www.ethicaljobs.com.au

EthicalJobs.com.au helps organisations that are making a difference to find passionate and committed staff by helping them to make more of a social and environmental impact through their activities. 27,000+ jobs posted in 12 months.

Jobs and Skills Centre Western Australia

- https://www.jobsandskills.wa.gov.au/jobs-and-skills-centre WA

Western Australia's TAFE Jobs and Skills Centres are one-stop shops for careers, training and employment advice and assistance. Services are free, and accessible to all members of the community. The centres are located on TAFE campuses throughout Perth and regional WA, with additional outreach locations for regional areas.

Each of the centres is staffed by people who can provide free professional and practical advice on training and employment opportunities including careers advice, apprenticeship and training information. Support services for employers and business, and specialist services for Aboriginal people, ex-offenders and people from a culturally or linguistically diverse background are also available.

Job Active Australian Job Searching

- https://jobsearch.gov.au/

Australian Public Service jobs

- https://www.apsjobs.gov.au/s/job-search

Airtasker – Self-employment opportunities

- www.airtasker.com

Popular job boards

- https://www.seek.com.au/
- https://www.careerone.com.au/
- https://www.glassdoor.com.au/

Apprenticeship support Australia

- http://www.apprenticeshipsupport.com.au/Home

Care Careers – for opportunities in the Care sector

- www.carecareers.com.au

NOTES

NOTES

NOTES

NOTES

www.ingramcontent.com/pod-product-compliance
Ingram Content Group UK Ltd.
Pitfield, Milton Keynes, MK11 3LW, UK
UKHW041637190726
13854UKWH00006B/2543